THE
WORDS
YOU NEED

by B Rudzka, J Channell, Y Putseys, P Ostyn

**MACMILLAN
PUBLISHERS**

First published 1981
Reprinted 1982, 1984, 1985, 1986, 1987, 1988, 1990 (three times), 1991,
1992, 1993, 1994

Published by MACMILLAN PUBLISHERS LTD
London and Basingstoke

ISBN 0–333–28150–0

Typeset by Activity, Teffont, Salisbury, Wilts
Printed in Hong Kong

Contents

Preface

The importance of words in verbal communication hardly needs stressing, yet no other language component has been more neglected in foreign language teaching than the lexicon. While a great deal of energy and imagination is going into the teaching of grammar, comparatively little is being done to teach words, and students of foreign languages, even after several years of strenuous effort, often know many grammatical frames but have very little to put into them.

The Words You Need, which this Teacher's Book accompanies, sets out specifically to organise the acquisition of language skills within the context of a structured approach to vocabulary teaching.

The approach used is a completely new one, adapting insights from theoretical linguistics and psycholinguistics to the service of the working language teacher. Once learnt it gives both teacher and student a systematic, clear and precise way of assimilating any further vocabulary they may come across.

In the Teacher's Book we try to answer the sort of questions teachers will want to ask. We explain the teaching methods used, and give practical guidance on the many and varied uses to which the material can be put. In order to make full use of this new material, the teacher may need some knowledge of the linguistic and pedagogic theories behind it. To this end, a brief introduction has also been included. We stress to those hard-pressed teachers who often turn past such pages to the practical ones, that *it is really essential for them to read this short theoretical section.*

Finally, we would like to add that there is no one right way to use this book. Our guidelines are meant only as suggestions, and the teacher has freedom to exploit the material in any way he pleases. We hope it will prove both enjoyable and worthwhile.

B Rudzka, J Channell, Y Putseys, P Ostyn

Introduction

1 Who is this book for?

This book is for post-intermediate and advanced students of English either as a
foreign or as a second language. By post-intermediate and advanced we mean for
example:
post-secondary students of English (ie those in Universities and Colleges)
students preparing for advanced academic study using English medium
trainee teachers of English at all levels
summer school students
students studying for Cambridge Proficiency or similar level exams
translators and interpreters
and generally any student who has reached the stage of adequate communication,
and wants to push his English towards a working equivalent of native speaker
English.

2 What should the student already know?

a   The basic grammatical structures of English. There is no explicit grammar
    teaching in this book, although a wealth of grammatically interesting material
    affords the teacher the opportunity to teach advanced grammar points from
    it, if he wishes.
b   A basic vocabulary of 2,000 to 2,500 words. Obviously the range of words
    known varies from student to student at this level, depending on the language
    he has encountered through course books and informal contact. Nevertheless
    we think most courses teach approximately the same range of functionally
    oriented vocabulary for day to day use up to this level.

3 Which words are presented?

The vocabulary taught covers a wide range of subjects and is designed to improve
the student's general level of communication, by giving him more words he can
use. For instance, he knows the general term **surprise**, and we add **astonish,
astound, amaze,** and **flabbergast.** We have excluded very unusual words, and those
having limited specialist uses.

4 What variety of English does the book teach?

English is spoken as a first language in many parts of the world and exists in many different varieties. It is also in wide use as a second and foreign language. It is obvious that Britain no longer has exclusive rights over dictating what is acceptable 'right' English. Nevertheless British English is widely accepted as an ideal standard towards which learners are guided. For this reason we have placed our emphasis on *standard British English*.

However, given the large volume of published material written in American English, which the student at this level cannot fail to meet, we have deliberately selected texts from both British and American sources. In marking the differences between American and British English we do not expect the student to master both varieties or be able to 'translate' from one to the other.What we do think necessary is for him to be able to understand both, and recognize the differences between them. The same is true for any non-standard English which occurs in some of our more colloquial texts.

For American English (referred to as *Am*) we have adopted the following system: all British spellings which are different from American spellings are listed on page ii of the Student's Book, and are not noted in individual texts. Differences of vocabulary and syntax are explained in the glosses. Since our emphasis is on British English (referred to as *Br*), we provide *Br* equivalents of *Am* expressions and words, but do not translate *Br* expressions into *Am*.

5 Why focus on vocabulary?

When a student has mastered the basic grammatical structures of English, he might well have a basic vocabulary of 1,500–2,500 words. What he needs to acquire at this stage is more words, words to put into the structures he knows. Usually he is told to 'go away and read as much as possible', the hope being that in some magic way exposure to large numbers of words will suddenly lead to rapid vocabulary extension. In this way, the student will probably learn to recognize new words, but is this sufficient? Let's look at some typical lexical errors which students make and with which all teachers are familiar.

The first type of error happens when the student has an idea of the basic sense of the words, but does not know:
a   which other words it will combine with (its *collocational properties*), or
b   how it relates to other words of similar meaning.
Here are a few examples:
*to put up a campaign
*she laughed broadly
*a good-looking view
*to estimate the evidence
(We follow the usual practice of marking an unacceptable expression or sentence with an *.)

Another common tendency among students is to overuse a limited set of words whose sense and collocational properties they are sure of. This results in a flat, uninteresting style and failure to express the variety of ideas they want to communicate, as in:
a good teacher/lesson/meal/day/girl/university

The third type of error arises from the student's erroneous (but natural) assumption that the collocational properties of a new word he has just met are the same as its translation equivalent in his own language. Here, his native language semantic competence interferes wih his English performance. For example, French speakers make the following errors:

*He closed the door with the key. (locked)
*a voyage by train (journey)
*I made an experience in the laboratory. (experiment)
*Whęn could I touch Mr Ostyn? (contact)
and Dutch speakers:
*You can easily overlook the several possibilities with their own value. (look at . . . at the same time)
*I sacked in mathematics. (failed).

When a student meets a new word either in a text or in conversation, he can usually only learn that it is correct in that context. If he looks it up in a dictionary he will find a definition, and perhaps some examples, but this won't help him much when he wants to know if it will be suitable in another context, nor will it help him to know how it relates to other words with similar meaning.

There are two things, besides basic sense, which a student needs to know about every new word he wants to make part of his active competence:
a   How does it relate to other words with similar meaning?
b   Which other words can it be used with, and in which contexts?

Linguistic theory and the language learner

Linguistics tries to provide a description of all the sentences of a language under investigation, which reflects the intuitions of its native speakers about when and how those sentences should be used. While the language learner is not, of course, consciously interested in 'providing a description' of the language he is learning, it is obvious that he must in some sense acquire all the information which would enable him to do so, since it is this same information which enables him to speak the language correctly. Given this similarity between the goals of the linguist, and those of the language learner, it is not surprising that some of the linguist's ways of investigating language are useful to the learner.

1 Semantic field theory

Particularly relevant to vocabulary acquisition is semantic field theory. This theory departs from the premise that the vocabulary of a language, far from being a random collection of words, consists of interrelating networks, made up of sets of semantically similar words. An example of a semantic field is the set of 'kinship terms': **mother, father, son, daughter, brother, sister, aunt, uncle**, etc. Clearly these words share some aspect of meaning which is not present in the item **cloud**. Another example of a field would be 'verbs of movement': **walk, run, stroll, amble, trot, jog.** But this field differs from kinship terms in the sense that here we may want to say that **stroll** is also part of another field consisting of **wander, stroll, roam, ramble.** Equally, **run** is a member of the field 'moving fast': **run, sprint, canter, gallop, dash.** It would be possible to go on assembling fields until we had covered the whole vocabulary of English, and we would want to place many words in perhaps two or three different fields. It is in this sense that vocabulary should be seen as a set of interrelating networks. By deploying this approach in teaching, we have at our disposal a systematic framework within which to present words to the learner.

2 Psychological validity

In addition to the practicality of this approach, there is evidence to show that the mind makes use of semantic similarity in finding words from memory for use in speech. Studies of slips of the tongue (ie when a speaker produces a wrong word, realises it, and corrects himself) made by native speakers of English have shown that many wrong words, far from being random mistakes, actually share some aspect of meaning with the intended word, for example:
I have my book and my **jigsaw** . . . I mean **crossword**
We **invited** him to . . . **asked** him to buy crisps
I really **like** to . . . **hate** to get up in the morning

Sometimes the 'wrong' word is a mixture of two words from the same semantic field:

I **swindged** (switched/changed)
momentaneous (instantaneous/momentary)
herrible (terrible/horrible) (Fromkin, 1973)

A second type of evidence comes from the speech of people with certain kinds of brain damage. In tests of reading, some of them, instead of saying the word they are shown, consistently say another word from the same semantic field, for example **canary** read as **parrot**, **ill** as **sick**, **city** as **town** and **bush** as **tree**. (Marshall and Newcombe, 1966)

This evidence suggests that the mind takes account of meaning in the way it stores and retrieves words. It may be that the mind stores words in the kind of semantic sets described above. If this is the case, it is clear that we should teach words in semantic fields in order to help students to remember them.

3 Componential analysis

Words belong to the same semantic field when they share some aspects of meaning but few words share all aspects. Synonymy is often a confusing rather than helpful notion to the student, since there are so few English words which are interchangeable in all contexts. For example, **run** and **sprint** are similar in both being verbs which express fast movement by human beings, but they differ in that **sprint** is used for a faster movement, over a short distance. Linguists describe such differences and similarities by breaking down the meaning of words into different pieces known as *semantic features*[1] (sometimes 'components', but we shall use 'features' throughout). For **run** and **sprint** this might be:

run: [+ move] [+ by feet] [+ quickly] [+ on land] [+ placing down one foot after another]
sprint: [+ move] [+ by feet] [+ as quickly as possible] [+ on land] [+ placing down one foot after another] [+ over a short distance]

Each feature is enclosed in a pair of square brackets. Note that they share some, but not all, features. This clear representation of differences and similarities between two words is exactly what the student learning new vocabulary needs.

4 Collocation

One of the main difficulties students encounter in relation to new items of vocabulary is knowing what their collocational properties are (which words they will go with), apart from the one collocation in which they have met the word. The most extreme version of collocational theory says that the meaning of a word

[1]Note that our presentation of semantic features departs considerably from that adopted by the specialist in semantics. Being interested in analysing the meaning of words, and not in teaching them, the semanticist employs one-word feature specifications. For teaching purposes, however, such specifications are not always suitable. The student is not likely to grasp the meaning of a word on the basis of a mere inventory of one-word features. It appears that at least some of the links between the features must be expressed verbally, and instead of one-word specifications we have often used whole phrases to elucidate areas of meaning.

Another departure from the usual practice of semanticists was to include in some of our semantic analyses information about syntactic constraints and the non-linguistic context in which words can be used.

is only accessible through its collocations. It is clear that for the student of English, an important aspect of knowing a word is knowing its collocational properties.

Language in use is very flexible, and the collocational possibilities of any word do not form a fixed set. That is to say, while English speakers agree on more typical collocations, there are many other collocations which some people would use, and others not, not to mention metaphorical and creative uses of language, which result in quite new collocations constantly being formed. A set of collocations is not therefore a list of all the ways in which a word can be used, but rather a set of examples of how a word is usually used. For the student, collocations are points of reference for him to use in forming his own collocations.

Used together, semantic field theory, componential analysis and the collocational approach give us a systematic, clear and precise way of presenting the vocabulary of English to students.

Organisation of the Student's Book

The Words You Need is made up of 20 Units each built around a different theme. Units 1–10 appear in Part 1, Units 11–20 in Part 2, which is a separate book. Each unit consists of:
Texts
Glosses
Discussion
Word Study
Exercises
It is conceived in two major sections, which correspond to Part 1 and Part 2. The words studied in each unit are repeatedly practised in subsequent exercises within each section. This means that a teacher may use Units 11–20 (Part 2) independently of Units 1–10 (Part 1) if he wishes.

1 Texts

The texts selected are all authentic.We have found that advanced students feel that specially written material in some sense talks down to them, and is not 'real' English. They far prefer authentic texts, even if they are a little more difficult.

Our selection covers a wide range of topics relevant not only in Britain and the USA, but worldwide, such as man's relation to his environment, health, psychic power, education, and work. We have tried as much as possible to avoid culture specific topics. No less varied are the style and the tone of expression, illustrating different degrees of formality and seriousness and at the same time satisfying different tastes and needs.

The texts are intended to serve a double purpose: to present students with challenging ideas and to provide a natural context of correct spoken and written English in which words can be learned.

2 Glosses

The selection of words for the glosses which accompany each text is based on our teaching experience with advanced students of different linguistic backgrounds, and given their varying requirements, we preferred to gloss too many words rather than too few. Therefore not all the glosses will be useful to all students. As an important aspect of vocabulary acquisition is learning to guess the meaning of unknown words from their context, we have not glossed those words whose sense is deduceable from the text. If necessary the student may, of course, check the accuracy of his 'guess' in a dictionary. In fact, we hope to encourage students to use monolingual dictionaries, and therefore our glosses are rather more indications of which meaning in the dictionary is the relevant one, than full definitions of the words concerned.

We do not, however, preclude the use of a bilingual dictionary for finding the names of birds, animals and plants, since we found that glossing these involved unnecessarily complicated, and not always very helpful, definitions.

3 Discussion

Our suggestions for discussion are not only an invitation to exchange ideas but also a pretext for using the words studied. Only when the student can use the words correctly and in a spontaneous way will the aim of the book have been fulfilled.

4 Word study

The following section is designed both to explain the Word Study section in the Student's Book and to guide the teacher in introducing it to his students (see also *Suggestions for using the book*).

Words are taught in semantic fields, or in contrastive pairs consisting of two members of a field. We single out words from our texts and add other words to make up a field. The semantic fields in any unit result directly from the vocabulary in the texts. This means that no field is introduced unless at least one of its members is illustrated in the texts of the unit in question. The remaining members of a given field are often drawn from texts presented in other units. This way of introducing words resembles the natural way a student would meet new vocabulary, experiencing it in situations, but has the added advantage of systematic explanation.

You will see that the Word Study of Unit 1 contains explanatory notes for the student. In addition the Word Study of Unit 1 is reprinted below, with further notes for the teacher (set in shaded boxes). The students' notes are very much simpler than the theoretical explanations in the Teacher's Book. We leave it to the teacher to judge how much of his theoretical knowledge he should pass on to any particular group of students. Once the students have worked through the Word Study of Unit 1 with the teacher, they will be able to study the Word Study in other units on their own, referring back if necessary to the guidance notes in Unit 1.

Word Study

This first Word Study contains guidance notes. All the other Word Study sections work in the same way as this one, and you will be able to study them by yourself. You can always refer back to the notes in this unit if you need to.

A Semantic Fields

A semantic field is a group of words which are similar in meaning. For example the words in the GRID below all describe a person having a good opinion of himself;

1 Opinions of oneself

	good opinion of oneself or what one has done		desire that others praise you to your face
	exaggerated	*or* justified	
conceit	+		
pride	+	+	
self-esteem		+	
vanity	+		+

The differences and similarities between the words are shown by the *semantic features* at the top of the grid. If there is a + against a word this means that the feature is part of the meaning of the word, so here, conceit and pride both include in their meaning [+ exaggerated good opinion of oneself] (Note that when we write features outside a grid we put them in square brackets with a + sign). If there is no +, either the feature is *not* part of the meaning of the word, or the feature does not help us to know the difference between the word and others in the field.

This grid is a simplified version of those usually made by semantic analysts — it uses only one sign +, instead of four or five, and its features are phrases rather than single words. The result is a grid which tells the learner exactly what he needs to know about the relationships between words in the field, by making explicit their differences and similarities.

Our grids are the result of consulting a number of dictionaries and native speakers. Where we found significant differences between different native speakers' judgements about words, we incorporated this by such markings as 'usually' or 'may imply . . . ' to show the student that he might meet uses of the word which are not in agreement with the given features.

8

Or between two features can mean two things:
If a word is marked for both the features, then both of them are part of its meaning, although not necessarily at the same time. **Pride** is such a word — in certain contexts it means that the good opinion of oneself is exaggerated and in others that it is justified.
If a word is marked for only one feature, the other one is *not* part of its meaning.

This scale shows how good or bad the qualities expressed by these words are:

good   bad

←——→

self-esteem   **pride**   **vanity**   **conceit**

This is not exact, of course, but it shows you that *vanity* is usually regarded as worse than *pride* which can have both a good and a bad sense.

We also use scales for other purposes. For example to compare intensity of feeling:

least   most

←——→

surprise   **astonish**   **amaze**   **astound**   **flabbergast**
(Unit 4)

or to make a stylistic comparison:

formal   informal   colloquial   slang

←——

steal   **steal**   **lift**   **swipe**   **rip off**
pilfer   **pinch**   **snitch**
(Unit 9)

The following adjectives are derived from these nouns: **conceited, proud** and **vain. Self-esteem** does not produce an adjective.
EXAMPLES
conceited   He is so **conceited** he can't imagine he might fail the exam.
proud   (positive sense) I am very **proud** of my garden this year.
    (negative sense) He is too **proud** to mix with the ordinary people in the village.
vain   Vain people like to be told nice things about themselves.

2 Counting up the worth

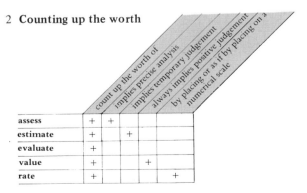

	count up the worth of	implies precise analysis	implies temporary judgement	always implies positive judgement or as if by placing on a	by placing or numerical scale
assess	+	+			
estimate	+		+		
evaluate	+				
value	+			+	
rate	+				+

Grammatical Explanation
Words in the same semantic field often also share grammatical properties. After each field, we give grammatical points about the words in the field.

All the above verbs, except **evaluate**, can appear in expressions of the type, to . . . . .sth at.
EXAMPLES
I would **estimate** my losses at $200.
His IQ is **rated** at 110.
The value of the house has been **assessed** at £ 25,000
Only **estimate** can be followed by a that-clause
EXAMPLE
We **estimated** that the work would take us two hours.

	sb's income for tax purposes	damages	the cost of sth (at)	the importance of sth	the evidence	sb's performance	sb's contribution to the debate	sb's ability	sb as very competent, highly capable, highly gifted	sb's property (at)	sb as a leader	sb's advice
assess	+	+	+	+	(+)	+	+	+				
estimate		+	+	+								
evaluate			+	+	+	+						
rate			(+)			+	(+)	+		+		
value						+	+			+	+	+

10

3 Forming judgements

	hint - or	form an opinion (about)	by imaginative deduction from given information	usu by careful and critical examination of facts	stresses idea of finality
conclude		+			+
infer	+	+	+		
judge		+		+	

These verbs are all transitive and can occur with the preposition **from** and a **that**-clause.

> **Verbal classification** The categories **transitive** and **intransitive** are used differently in different books. We have adopted the following distinctions. If a verb can be used with no object of any kind, it is described as **intransitive**.
> EXAMPLES
> He is crawling   She goes out
> She cried   We will go there tomorrow
> If it takes an object noun, pronoun, participle or infinitive, an object introduced by a preposition, or a sentential object, it is said to be **transitive**.
> EXAMPLES
> He bought a book   I thought of my sister
> He said nothing   I threw out all my old letters
> I like her   He asked when we would come back
> I like swimming   He said that he would come with us
> I like to swim
>
> In cases where the nature of the verbs is obvious, no comment is given.

EXAMPLES
conclude   Am I to **conclude** from your criticism that you intend to leave your job?
infer   They **inferred** from his behaviour that he no longer wished to be friends with them.
judge   From all I know of her, I would **judge** that she will make an excellent mother.
Judge is more common, however, with a direct object followed by an adjective and/or a **to**-infinitive.
EXAMPLES
I would **judge** him to be a first-rate linguist.
Would you **judge** it necessary to read all the books on the reading list?
They will **judge** him overqualified for the job, I am afraid.

4 Being dirty

dirty		
filthy	grimy	grubby

These words are related to each other in a way which can be explained by a diagram. The word at the top is more general, and the ones below are different kinds of **dirty**.

	covered with dust, soil, mud, etc	disgusting	dirt covering surface	dirt rubbed onto or into surface	result of human contact
dirty	+				
filthy	+	+			
grimy	+		+		
grubby	+		+	+	+

The words also differ in the amount of dirt implied:

not very   very

←——————————————————————————————→

                      dirty   **grimy**   **filthy**

                                           grubby

	man	family	dog	house	windows	clothes	hands	face	streets	water	language	joke	mind	trick	business
dirty	+	+	+	+	+	+	+	+	+	+	+	+	+	+	+
filthy		+		+	+			+	+	+	+	+			
grimy		(+)	+	+	+	(+)	+								
grubby						+	+	+							

Notice that **dirty** and **filthy** are frequently employed figuratively to mean 'vulgar' or 'immoral'.

5 Being attractive

	making a pleasant impression on the senses	close to an ideal	worthy of being loved	suggests relative smallness	suggests femininity or delicacy	arousing interest	causing pleasure	suggests lightness and grace	suggests having good manners	may suggest sexual attraction	having well proportioned features / or well made or of good quality	often suggests strength / or suggests dignity	result of great generosity
beautiful	+	+											
lovely	+		+										
pretty	+			+	+	~							
charming	+				+	+	+	+					
attractive	+					+				+			
good-looking	+								.		+		
handsome	+									+	+	+	+

In this grid, **or** occurs alone in a box. It introduces a feature which is not in contrast with the one immediately before it. It is in contrast with an earlier feature presenting a basic sense. For example, [+ result of great generosity] is in contrast with [+ making a pleasant expression on the senses] and *not* with [+ may suggest sexual attraction].

When qualifying people, **good-looking** and **handsome** are more often used for men, and **lovely, beautiful** and **pretty** for women. **Attractive** may be used for either. When qualifying inanimate and abstract nouns, there is often little semantic distinction between **beautiful, lovely, charming** and **attractive**.

	woman	man	child	dog	bird	flower	weather	landscape	view	day	village	house	furniture	bed	picture	dress	present	voice	proposal
beautiful	+		+	+	+	+	+	+	+	+	+	+	+	+	+	+	+	+	
lovely	+		+	(+)		+	+		+	+	+	+	+	(+)	+	+	+	+	
pretty	+		+		+	+			+	+			+	+	+				
charming	+	+	+						+	+							+		
attractive	+	+							+	+					+		+		+
good-looking	+	+	+	+															
handsome	+	+													+				

13

In speech, **beautiful, lovely, charming** and **attractive** are often used for situations in which their real meaning would be too strong, in order to express enthusiasm.

EXAMPLES

The walls were covered with a most
| beautiful |
| lovely |
| charming |
| attractive |
wall paper.

I'll come to see you at about seven — will you be there?
Beautiful — okay — see you later.
She does really **lovely** things for people like bringing them their favourite flowers on their birthday.
Bacon and eggs for breakfast! **Lovely!**

6 Having a good appearance

	graceful *or*	formal and fashionable *or*	showing good taste *or*	fashionable *or*	formally dressed *or*	clean and tidy	showing great attention to small details of one's appearance	usu of women only
elegant	+	+	+					
smart				+	+	+		
well–dressed				+	+			
well–groomed						+	+	+

Note that it is not necessary for all the words in a semantic field to share a single feature. In such cases, it is the similarity of features which brings the words together.

Smart, when it means [+ clean and tidy] or [+ formally dressed] is colloquial.

EXAMPLES
elegant   She dismissed him with an **elegant** wave of her hand.
The most **elegant** clothes are often the most simple, but usually also the most expensive.
Fiona manages to look **elegant** even in riding clothes.
Clothes by a new young designer are suddenly to be seen at all the season's most **elegant** occasions.
smart   One of my favourite amusements is to sit in a **smart** restaurant in the centre of town and watch the famous and elegant people one sees there.
Should I put on something **smart** to go out to the Browns'?
Judith always looks so **smart,** she makes me feel very untidy.
well-dressed   You can always tell a really **well-dressed** man by his shoes.
It is important to be **well-dressed** when one goes for a job interview.
well-groomed   No **well-groomed** woman ever goes out without checking her make-up in the mirror.
What I tend to notice more about a woman than her clothes is whether or not she is **well-groomed.**

14

B Synonymous Pairs

As we have said, there are few words completely the same in meaning. 'Synonymous' is taken to mean 'very similar in meaning'.

In this section, you will find pairs of words similar in meaning, with an explanation of the difference between them.

1 **work**
   task   [+ piece of] [+ usu assigned]

When one member of a pair can be explained in terms of the other, we mention the features of the more specific word which make it different from the more general word. For example, here, a task is a 'piece of work, usually assigned'.

	a task	work	someone's work
to do		+	+
to perform	+		
to set	+	+	

2 **situation**
   plight   [+ bad]

EXAMPLE
With no documents and no money in a country where she didn't even speak the language, she was in a terrible **plight**.

3 **to produce**
   to generate   [+ energy, force] ⇒ [+ be the cause of] [+ usu a state of mind]

An arrow (⇒) indicates the metaphorical, figurative sense.
For example, the literal sense of **generate** is 'to produce energy', as in:
The hydro-electric scheme **generates** enough power for the whole city.
Used figuratively it means 'to cause' as in:
The government's policy towards immigrants has **generated** a lot of hostility.

	electricity	wrong attitudes	hostility	heat	ideas	milk	food	plays	films	effects
produce			+	+	+	+	+	+	+	
generate	+	+	+	+	+					

4 **to speak**
   to mutter   [+ in a low voice] [+ indistinctly]

EXAMPLE
He came home in a bad mood, **muttered** something about coming back later, and I haven't seen him since.

5 unpleasant, unattractive

ghastly   [+ intensely] ; often used in colloquial speech and writing to express strong dislike. It is not used in this sense in formal speech and writing.

EXAMPLES

a	**ghastly**	job dinner party film dress book lecture boyfriend

6 unwilling
reluctant

Unwilling and **reluctant** are synonymous when used attributively; for instance, both **an unwilling helper** and **a reluctant helper** denote someone who helps but does not want to.

When used predicatively, however, **unwilling** means 'not doing' and **reluctant** means 'not wanting to do'.

EXAMPLES

He was **unwilling** to give any information. This means that he did not give any information.

He was **reluctant** to give any information. This implies that he did give information but without wanting to.

7 open
overt   [+ of actions, attitudes] [+ to be noticed]

	person	house	window	letter	hostility	hatred	threat	declaration	proposal	beliefs
open	+	+	+	+	+	(+)	+	+		
overt					+	+	+	+	+	+

8 profitable
lucrative   [+ bringing in a lot of money]

	arrangement	experience	discovery	business	deal	profession	trade	occupation
profitable	+	+	+	+	+			
lucrative			+	+	+	+	+	

16

9 carefully
  conscientiously   [+ guided by one's sense of what is right]

	carefully	conscientiously
to drive	+	
to observe the rules	+	
to describe sth	+	
to work	+	+
to look after one's children	+	+
to inspect sth	+	+
to care for one's patients	+	+
to fulfil one's obligations		+

5 Exercises

An important aspect of learning new words is the opportunity to practise them.
Our emphasis is on systematic repetition of words by means of different types of
exercises. Each unit (except Unit 1) contains two sorts of exercises:
a   exercises which practise the words and expressions used in the texts and
    Word Study of the unit
b   revision exercises which offer further practice of words from preceding
    units.
  The student is now aware of the concepts of field theory, componential
analysis and collocation, so his knowledge of the meaning and collocations of particular words is reinforced by exercises specially designed to reflect these
concepts.
Examples of these are:

1 What are the similarities and differences between the following pairs?
1 to see sth/to look at sth   2 to surprise/to astonish   3 to pour tea/to spill tea
4 an ability/a skill   5 paint/varnish   6 a target/a goal

This exercise requires the student to make an informal feature analysis of the
words in each pair.

2 Choose from the words in brackets the one which best fits the given context.
1   In London you see tramps . . . . the street, looking for something and
     looking for nothing. (**roam, walk, go**)
2   As we reached the top of the hill a . . . . .view stretched out before us.
     (**good-looking, handsome, beautiful**)

This tests collocational competence, and also the student's knowledge of how
words in a field relate to each other.

3 What can you . . . .?
1 be fed up with   2 be horrified by   3 overlook   4 discriminate against

This tests collocational competence.

In addition, there are exercises designed to expand the student's awareness of the interaction of linguistic and contextual factors, eg

4 Consider the following words and give as many contextual details as you can.
1 to trudge   2 to amend   3 to smack   4 to intercept   5 to mature
6 stereotype

Other exercises invite the student to reflect on the figurative use or on the stylistic properties of words.

There are exercises asking for summaries of texts including specific words, for definitions of words, and for creative writing following the style and vocabulary of example texts.

We also have continuous pieces of prose in which the students must fit logical and contextually suitable words from a given list. This encourages sensitivity to context. Finally, crosswords provide a more relaxing practice of the words learnt.

All these exercises aim specifically at helping the student to avoid the kind of lack of precision and over-generalization which so often characterizes his speech.

Suggestions for using the book

1 The texts and topics for discussion

The texts presented in our book vary considerably in form and content and as such lend themselves to a wide variety of uses. At the outset, we would like to dissuade you from following a practice which is still quite common among teachers, at least in our part of the world. What we have in mind is the practice of reading aloud each text in class. Your time is far too precious to be spent on activities which the student can effectively carry out on his own. We suggest, however, that you teach the words posing pronunciation problems. You will find them listed at the end of this book.

When asking the students to prepare the texts, point out to them that they will remember the words better if the texts are re-read at one or two day intervals. Whereas they need to go over *all* the texts, you may well prefer to devote class time to the close study of one or two in particular.

There are many ways of handling a text and you should try to vary your approach from lesson to lesson. Here are a few suggestions. In addition to the well-known practices of you or the students asking questions on the texts or the students summarizing the texts, you could get them to concentrate on the style or kind of English used. For example, you could conduct a search for the main characteristics of American English in texts such as 'Advertising Can Sell You Anything' (Unit 4), 'Getting Involved' (Unit 9), or 'A Walk Across America' (Unit 10). In turn, articles from *The Sunday Post, Honey* or *Weekend* (some of which are included in Units 1, 5, 11 and Units 17, 18 in Part 2) may lead to interesting observations on colloquial English as distinct from formal English. The latter type of English is illustrated in such articles as 'Pretty Pleases' (Unit 1), 'The Social Order of Japanese Macaques' (Unit 3), 'The Computer and Privacy' (Unit 12, Part 2), 'Cultural Concepts of Time' (Unit 13, Part 2) and 'Crime and Punishment' (Unit 18, Part 2).

Another activity for which the texts may serve as a springboard is role playing. Depending on the subject matter, you divide the class into pairs, assigning the roles of journalist and scientist, doctor and resuscitated patient, fortune teller and client, interviewer and cross-continental walker, and so on. For the sake of variety, you assign to a third student the role of a reporter who listens in on the conversation between the other two and summarizes what was said, or, a good exercise for prospective teachers, makes a note of mistakes.

Many of the texts can also be used as a starting point for discussion. Like role playing, discussions are most effective when carried out in small groups. Therefore, we strongly recommend that you divide the class into groups of 3–4 students, ensuring that there is a good student in each group to guide the conversation. As students often do not know how to start a discussion, they may want to use our lists of topics. If, however, they feel inspired, they should follow their own line of interest. The important thing is that they engage in a spontaneous exchange of ideas. In order not to stifle spontaneity or inhibit the more timid, we suggest that you do not correct their mistakes immediately. (You may take notes and comment on them at the end of the lesson). It is imperative, however, that you show your interest in what they are doing by supplying unknown words, introducing new ideas or stimulating the discussion by making controversial statements. Each of the groups may, of course, talk about something different. In fact, we often divide our students according to what they want to discuss. They obviously feel more at ease with topics of their own choice. Incidentally, we have found out that they express themselves more effectively and derive greater enjoyment from the discussion when they prepare the topics in advance. This preparation usually involves a close reading of our lists of suggestions for discussion and grouping words relevant to a given topic. Some students are very keen on jotting down beforehand what they intend to say.

From time to time the whole class may wish to have a discussion. One way of organizing such a general discussion is to let students take turns in asking and answering questions or in reporting on personal experience. Our own students had very successful discussion sessions of this kind on the texts about psychic power and discrimination against women.

Whichever of the activities suggested you choose, bear in mind that variety is the best way of maintaining the students' interest. It may therefore be advisable to spend no more than 20–30 minutes on activities revolving around the texts, unless the students become engaged in a very lively discussion.

2 The word study sections

As the presentation of words in componential and collocational grids is new, a few guidelines on how to tackle them are in order. We start with the notion of semantic field and semantic feature. One way of introducing the idea of semantic fields to students is the following:

a   Books open at the first text in Unit 1 'Body Image'.

b   Do *not* ask the students to look at Grid 5 until the end of this exercise. Start with the word **beautiful**. Ask the students to think of, or find in the text, other words of similar meaning. Each time a student suggests a word, ask him why he thinks it is similar to **beautiful**. Ask the others if they agree. If they do, write it on the board with **beautiful**. Continue until all the words in semantic field no. 5 have been assembled (you may have to provide some of them). Tell the students that a group of similar meaning words like this is called a semantic field.

c   Next, ask them to tell you the differences between the words in the field: Is **pretty** the same as **charming**? What is the difference between 'an attractive man' and 'a good looking man'? In this way the students will make (orally) an informal feature analysis. Then ask them to give examples of nouns which these adjectives typically go with. You may need to use the collocational grid to check their suggestions.

d   Finally, ask them to turn to Grid 5, and show them how it sets out visually the sort of points they have just been making orally. Explain the collocational grid (you will need to explain the word *collocate*) and show how it could be expanded to include any additional examples they may have made.

While commenting on the grids, make use of the special instructions on Unit 1 printed on p 7–18 of this book. It will often happen that you need to draw the students' attention to the syntactic and stylistic properties of words in a given field. You will also have to make them aware of false cognates; in Unit 1 **self-conscious** is a dangerous false cognate for Romance speakers, as the cognate in those languages stands for a virtue, and has the same meaning as the English **self-aware.**

Once your students become familiar with the mechanism of analysing words into smaller units of meaning, we suggest that you do not discuss every single part of the word study in class. Ask the students to read the section at home and mark anything that is not quite clear to them. When you next meet, go over the points that caused problems and encourage the students to go back to the word study each time they encounter a difficulty in an exercise. Encourage them also to re-read in a systematic fashion the example sentences which accompany the grids. This will enable them not only to master the meaning of the words illustrated but also to grasp the situations in which they can be used.

3 The exercises

After the students have worked their way through the texts and the word study, they can start on the exercises. Once more, the number of exercises covered in class will largely depend on the type of student you are working with and the time allotted. In any case, we suggest that your students prepare the exercises beforehand. In view of the considerable time this will require, they should not be expected to prepare both the new and revision exercises for the same lesson.

You will have noticed that some of our exercises call for filling in all sorts of grids or finding words that fit a given definition. When going over them in class, allow only short answer periods. The student should be able to give an immediate answer; if he hesitates, then he does not know the words concerned and should be asked to study them again. He can do this easily by referring to the relevant gloss, grid or synonymous pair. Note that we do *not* expect the student to know everything that is in the grids by heart. Rather, we expect him to consult the grids as often as possible, and we use some of the more mechanical fill-in exercises as a pretext to oblige him to do so.

In addition to giving vocabulary practice, the exercises mentioned can be fun, particularly when done orally and at high speed. You can even have a game in which the students compete in two groups for the best and quickest answers.

The exercises that require more reflection and allow for variation in responses, for example Exs. 2.8, 2.9, 2.10, 2.11, 3.1, 3.6, 3.13, 4.1, and 11.13, 12.13 in Part 2 can be successfully combined with small-group discussions. The students could compare and evaluate each other's answers and justify their choice of synonyms, semantic features, descriptive details, etc. The need to justify one's choice is especially felt when students are asked to fill in blanks in continuous pieces of prose, to complete sentences with synonymous expressions or to describe the situation in which a given word can or must be used.

While helping the students to retain the words, all these group exercises afford practice in self-expression and precision. Obviously, certain students will need this kind of practice more than others, and you could provide it at the cost of some of the easier exercises. Feel free to omit whatever you consider less useful or relevant to your students. It may be of interest to you to learn that in the case of some Dutch speaking students our derivational exercises turned out to be less important and could be dropped altogether, yet according to reports from the University of Trier, they posed a serious problem for German speaking students.

In order to let the students practise new words in written form, we have included a few exercises requiring summaries of texts or creative writing. Many of our discussion topics can also be used for written assignments.

Some of the written exercises, eg those asking the student to make up a questionnaire, a description of himself or a job advertisement, could be tackled in class. They can be quite effective when combined with conversation. On the contrary, the time needed for written completion exercises, such as 3.2, 3.10, 4.7, 4.8 and 5.2, will be spent more effectively if students do them at home and concentrate in class on comparing and justifying their answers.

All the techniques mentioned above hold for the new as well as the revision exercises. The revision exercises can, moreover, be conveniently used as informal tests. These tests might consist of only a few items, yet when administered frequently and unexpectedly, they will certainly stimulate the students to work systematically. The students could be told that there is no point in constantly covering new material if little of it is being retained, and that the idea of the test is to help them to see how much of the earlier material they still know and to refresh their memories.

4 Class time

It will be clear by now that the material of each unit is readily adaptable to class periods of varying duration and can be broken up and tackled on different days.

Assuming you are at Unit 3, you may do in class selected revision exercises from Unit 2, then organise a 20–30 minute discussion or role playing or question-and-answer period around the texts of Unit 3. The last 15 minutes could be spent on problems from the word study section of Unit 3. If you teach 90-minute periods, you will still have time for some new exercises from Unit 3.

An alternative approach would be to start with a few revision exercises from Unit 2, then pass on to the word study of Unit 3, backtrack to the texts of Unit 3, and finish with a discussion on the topics accompanying them. If you do not have the time to do the new exercises of Unit 3, you can do them at the beginning of the next lesson, before you start work on the texts of the Word Study of Unit 4.

We would like to stress once more that what this teachers' guide offers is only suggestions. You will undoubtedly find your own way of using the book to its best advantage.

Words posing pronunciation problems, listed by unit and text

Unit 1
Body image psychology, toward, Seneca, advertisement, ideals, deluge, worthy, acknowledged, seconded, soul, jealousy, average, obviously, attributes, accurate, assertive, charismatic
Pretty pleases cues, stature, behavioral, targets, determine, ascertain, stimulus, stereotyped inferences, pursuing, plight
Image-builder image, colleague, grimy

Unit 2
Nuclear energy fission, incredible, liabilities, tissues, tearing, dosage, genetic, strontium, whatever, earthquakes, riots, menace
Population bomb bomb, figures, Christ, assert, respite, colossal, environmental, fertile, pesticides, acres, efficacious, monoxide
Democracy euphoria, carcinogenic, primordial, undeniably, mutagenic
Future in futurism inherent, determined, epoch, famine, shrewdly, National Enquirer's, gauge, psychic, schedule, maniac, genius, foreign, purgatory

Unit 3
Social order macaques, threaten, hierarchy, analogous, canine, ethologist, predator
Jackdaws genuinely, assent, betrothal, betrothed, feathers, solicitous
Instinct alert, termites, penduline, knot, plaited, delicate, bowerbirds, esthetic, prodigious, baubles, conquest
Language of parrots colonel, hoopoes
Value of dog akin, enliven, severing, yearning, dreary
Koala explosion endearing, slaughtered, eucalyptus, lounge, gusto
A rare sight crouch, stoats, whistling, burial

Unit 4
Equality haunt, civilization, heir, sphere, era, knowledgeable
Advertising deliberate, diapers, gimmickry
Consumer resistence austere, graduate, Michigan, huge
Come closer mascaras, superlustre
Ads malt, liquor, gelatin, ginger ale

Unit 5
Family giddy, widespread, plagued
Spare the rod cajole, steady, courtesy, household chores, equanimity
Child a bully Goliath, hero, bully, victimisation
Childhood infantilism, infantilizing, allegedly, evils
Trouble ruefully, at loggerheads with, reckon, row (quarrel), financial

Unit 6

Parkinson's law subordinates, vacancy, concurrence, idle, wry, bowed
New ways to work nude, vacation, typist, bogus, provocative, sabotage,
humanitarian, Seattle, design, sauna, leisure, health
A youthful frivolity leading, Humphrey Berkeley, Cambridge, Selhurst,
headmaster, H. Rochester Sneath, fictitious, centenary, architect, Harrow,
involved, entitled
Career tips counselor, elite, managerial, non-glamorous locales, be wary, altern-
atives, major, weighing
Ludicrous executive, foreman

Unit 7

Why love? realm, alienate
Changing patterns deviance, juvenile, research, alcohol, privacy, jealousy, furtive,
determinant, indefinitely
Letters bowl, secure, wallow, tuition
Any offers? asylum

Unit 8

Search for psychic power intuitive, canister, psychometrist, bipolar, luminous,
insulate, Detroit, ironically
Shock from a gipsy sovereigns
Ever seen a ghost? meningitis, diagnose
Life after death? exhibited, tunnel, resuscitate, psychiatrists, psychologists,
heightened, near-death, pervasive, wholeness, limbs, benign, morphine, ambiguity
I used to be a man crusades, coincide, astrologer, virgo, awkward
Lord Luck sagittarius, aquarius, aries, taurus, gemini
Spot cheque herald

Unit 9

Explosive growth urbanisation, upheaval, gigantic, dubious, avalanche, millenia,
deluge
Problems of cities memoirs, germ, automobile, noxious, ghetto, prowlers, bemoan
City monkeys rhesus, niches, foraging, elaborate
Getting involved tedious, homesteader, nudging, horizon, endeavors, guy, plow,
plumbers, electrician, masons, veterinarian, morel, mushrooms

Unit 10

Walk across America Connecticut, Allegheny, Carlisle, hawks, muscles, breath,
Appalachians, ruby (light), hoarse, vegetarian, North Carolina, sweaty, shaky-
kneed, Lloyd, Mount Zion Baptist Church, deacon, pew, gut wrenching, Chatta-
hoochee, wilderness, commune, magnetizing, Lewis County, Martian, dawdle,
tomatoes, buoy, Mobile, azaleas, enamored, New Orleans

Key to the exercises

Unit 1

1 1 neglect 2 look down on 3 departure 4 shallow 5 ugly, hideous 6 irrelevant 7 unsure 8 reluctantly

2 1 [+ having ability, knowledge, or skill] 2 [+ over-high opinion of oneself] 3 [+ of men] 4 [+ in a low voice] [+ indistinct] 5 [+ insisting on one's rights] 6 [+ covered with dirt] 7 [+ place on a numerical scale] 8 [+ appointments] [+ with members of the opposite sex] 9 [+ guided by one's sense of what is right] 10 [+ shy]

3 1 a person one does not know 2 set of steps joined by two long pieces usually of wood or metal, used for climbing up and down 3 a shelter from which one can telephone 4 the hair growing on the ridge above the eye 5 place where commercial aeroplanes land and take off 6 difficult or sad situation or condition 7 is not important 8 become more important in the eyes of others or become physically stronger and more muscular 9 hours of the day when most people are travelling to or from work

4 1 a window, glass, ice, illusions, hopes 2 a parcel, box, jar, packet, bottle, suitcase, trunk 3 a letter, parcel, packet, post-card 4 papers, documents, letters, application forms 5 a response, information, an answer 6 a letter, parcel, packet, post-card 7 an ambition, goal, an aim, a target, an increase 8 danger, difficulty, situation, one's point of view, sb's attitude 9 a letter, parcel, packet, post-card 10 one's teeth, one's hair, one's nails, one's clothes 11 anything in the future 12 milk, beer, water, wine, apples, papers 13 electricity, heat, friction

5 1 advertisement 2 relation(ship) 3 finding 4 settlement 5 appearance 6 interaction 7 application 8 respondent, response 9 assessment 10 departure 11 assistance, assistant 12 interference

6 1 a person who you think less good than yourself. Example answers: poor people, rich people, lazy people, right wing politicians, left wing politicians, strikers, manual workers, students, women, men
2 anything frightening, or very serious. Examples: an accident, an injured person, violence, killing, drug-taking, the number of deaths on the road
3 an error, a fault, a mistake, sth sb has done wrong
4 receipt of a letter, a parcel
5 a person or persons from a group, usually a minority (in a society), who the society thinks inferior.
6 your voice, your appearance, success, failure, your work, your sex life, a sport
7 a god, sb's ability to succeed, a political movement
8 any person: a friend, a teacher, a student, an old lady; or some large object: a door, a tree, a lamp post, a bicycle

9 advice, help, good teaching, a change, a rest, a holiday
10 other people's feelings/needs/wants, an atmosphere in a group of people, other people's opinions/beliefs
11 one's goals, knowledge, success, a course of action, one's studies, a career

7   These are guidance notes about the content of answers for the teacher. The student may present his answer in any acceptable form of English sentence:
   1 similar   both connected with perception by the eye
     different **look at** implies deliberate action to try to perceive
             see implies success in perception
   2 similar   both mean to take something from an existing text
     different **summarize** is to make shorter to explain the main points
             copy is to reproduce the whole text
   3 similar   in both, the subject takes the place of the object
     different **supersede** implies that the subject is better, and in many cases, newer than what it replaces
   4 similar   tea moves from teapot to somewhere else
     different **pour**   tea goes into cup or other container
             spill   tea goes accidentally on floor, table, clothes, not in container
   5 similar   close examination of sth, part by part
     different **analyse**   provide description and explanation as well
   6 similar   about future event
     different **wait for**   you know event will happen
             expect   you think it will happen
   7 similar   both denote a person different from you
     different **foreigner**   from another country
             stranger   person you don't know
   8 similar   both refer to a condition or state of affairs
     different **plight** is always bad
   9 similar   both present a visual image on a flat surface
     different **a painting** must be produced by hand application of coloured substances

8   1 self esteem   2 dissect   3 eyelashes or lashes   4 results, findings
   5 shatter   6 bright   7 edge up (close) to   8 supersede   9 wig

9   1 stamped addressed envelope or self-sealing envelope   2 form   3 goals
   4 ladder   5 from   6 below   7 better/worse   8 pencil   9 shattered
   10 bad   11 elicited

10   1 similar   all are measures of length
     different **inch** and **yard** are non-metric, 1 inch = 2.5 cm approx., 1 yard = 90 cm approx.
   2 similar   connected with eyes
     different **eyeshadow** is a cosmetic preparation put around eyes to make them look nice; **eyelashes** are the hairs on the edge of the eyelid
   3 similar   both are things one must do, usually work
     different **a task** is one piece of work, assigned
             duty is work you feel you should do, and others expect you to do

4 similar   both join one thing to another, eg ideas, events
  different in the literal sense, **link** forms part of a chain
5 similar   both for storing things
  different **a shelf** is a flat, narrow piece of wood, **a cupboard** is closed
            and has a door
6 similar   both concern what one can do
  different **skill** is the ability to do something well
7 different a **collar** is part of a dress, coat or shirt, that fits round the
            neck
8 similar   something one aims in a sporting game, by extension,
            something one wants to achieve in the future
  different **target** is a round object to shoot at
            goal consists of two posts between which the ball must pass
            to score in the game of football
9 similar   both mean not clean
  different **scruffy** includes dirty but also old and worn (of clothes)

11 1 condition, especially a bad one, eg to be in a sad plight
      2 to speak in a low, indistinct voice; to murmer, to grumble
      3 profitable, bringing in money
      4 a dog of no special breed or of mixed breed
      5 the part of a dress or shirt that fits round the neck
      6 experiencing contradictory and opposing emotions toward the same
        person at the same time, especially love and hate
      7 characteristics, distinguising marks
      8 causing horror, terror or fear, as in a ghastly accident; pale, deathlike,
        as to look ghastly; very bad or unpleasant *coll*, eg a ghastly dinner
      9 unwilling, not wanting to do sth
      10 find out, discover, eg it was not easy to ascertain what had happened
      11 done openly or publicly, not secretly

12 1 seconded   2 mirror   3 overwhelming   4 jealous   5 embarrassed
      6 traits   7 target   8 blameworthy   9 egotistical   10 favour

Unit 2

1 1 an irresponsible act   2 a complex/complicated/intricate device   3 an
      inadequate description   4 a developing country   5 an invalid/spurious
      statement   6 a decreasing/declining birth rate   7 an undernourished/a
      starving child   8 a credible/believable/plausible story

2 1 complacency   2 depth   3 ferocity   4 shortage   5 nourishment
      6 fertilizer   7 pollution   8 consumption   9 dwelling   10 assumption
      11 perception   12 democracy   13 growth   14 cruelty

3 1 [+ dangerous]   2 [+ attract]   3 [+ cruel]   4 [+well-based]
      5 [+ not worry about consequences]   6 [+ permanent quality of]
      7 [+ be enough]   8 [+ peace] [+ calm]   9 [+ cause to disappear]

4 1   plants, trees, flowers, a project, a business, a school
      2   conditions, an illness, the weather, noise, relations between people/
          countries, a shortage
      3   any container for liquid — tank, bowl, reservoir, barrel; roof, wall

4 food, drink
5 smoke, dust, a soft cushion or cloth
6 problems, puzzles, scientific phenomena, UFO's, crimes, mysteries
7 the ground, the earth, a person, a building
8 nuclear power, floods, hurricanes, tornados
9 insects, pests, diseases
10 the sky, the weather
11 people
12 food, cars, furniture, money, weather, clothes, garments

5   1 succeed   2 announce   3 extrapolate   4 destroy   5 observe
     6 apply   7 endanger   8 reduce   9 assert

6   1 screen   2 famine   3 scope   4 dam   5 flourishing   6 gauge
     7 deteriorated   8 random   9 fertile   10 resolve

7   1 poisonous   2 truthful   3 shrewd   4 conceptual   5 hazardous
     6 efficacious   7 impressive   8 endless   9 comparative   10 doubtful,
     doubtless   11 numerous   12 utopian

8   1 triggered off   2 inquire   3 reluctant   4 prevent   5 baffles
     6 trivial   7 inscrutable   8 responsive   9 current   10 shattered

9   1 an engine, a car, a machine, a nuclear reactor, a generator
     2 riot, rebellion, protest, revolution, social change
     3 knowledge, information
     4 death, danger, enemies, heights
     5 water power, electric power, steam
     6 fields, plantations, the desert, gardens
     7 towns, villages, buildings, planes, crops, forests, vegetation
     8 books, articles, notices, a thesis, newspapers, magazines, journals
     9 rainfall; liquid (in a container) eg oil, petrol, water, fat, chemicals;
        temperature, pressure
    10 an attempt to do sth, a complaint, a disaster, a tragedy, a difficult
        situation

10   1 similar   both are planes
        different   the first is driven by a petrol engine and has propellers,
                    whereas the second is powered by jet engines
     2 similar   both refer to lists giving times when things will happen
        different   a **schedule** is usually for events which only happen once,
                    whereas a **timetable** is for recurring events, eg train or
                    plane departures
     3 similar   both connected with lack of food
        different   **hunger** is feeling one wants to eat something, whereas
                    famine is a complete lack of food anywhere
     4 similar   all are collections of houses where people live
        different   a **city** is a large and important town, a **village** is a small
                    group of houses in the country, smaller than a town
     5 similar   both are bad events
        different   a **misfortune** happens to an individual or small group of
                    people whereas a **catastrophe** is a sudden disaster affecting
                    large numbers of people

6 similar   all are clouds on the landsurface which make seeing difficult
   different   **smog** is fog mixed with smoke, **mist** is thinner than fog
7 similar   all are used when men fight each other
   different   **weapon** is the general term for anything used in fighting, a
   gun fires a metal projectile, a **bomb** is a device designed to
   explode once at a given time, and a **bullet** is used in the
   type of gun designed for shooting at and by individuals
8 similar   both connected with feeling contented about life
   different   **euphoria** implies the person does not realise or notice when
   things are wrong
9 similar   both connected with satisfaction with a state of affairs
   different   **self-confidence** is belief in one's own ability, **complacency**
   is belief that things are good and cannot be improved
10 similar   both are direct descendants
   different   **children** are born of you, **offspring** are born of your
   children or their children
11 similar   **responsibility** is what you are supposed to do, **liability** is
   what you must do in law
12 similar   both concern aggression between groups of people
   different   a **riot** is short and not organised, whereas a **war** is organised
   and uses weapons
13 similar   both are ways of seeing
   different   a **glimpse** is a quick look
14 similar   all tell the future
   different   a **forecast** is a statement of likely future events, based on
   analysis of relevant facts; a **prediction** may be based on
   analysis or not; a **prophecy** is usually magically inspired
15 similar   both concern a break or discontinuity
   different   **lag** is only for falling behind in time, **gap** is also for an
   opening, or space between two objects
16 similar   both used for feeding growing plants
   different   **fertilizer** is artificially produced, **manure** is the natural
   excreta of animals
17 similar   both designate the surface of the earth
   different   **ground** is the surface, **soil** is one type of surface, that in
   which cultivated plants can grow

11   1   change, worsening, improvement, development, deterioration, death, building-up
     2   machine, means of travel, storage place, means of disposal, method, machine, nuclear reactor
     3   substance, food, chemical, smoke
     4   substance, food, chemical process, bi-product, change, experience
     5   journey, climb, rescue, undertaking, drive, enterprise, business
     6   facts, processes, people, animals, test results, machines
     7   missile, weather-forecast, prediction, spy-plane
     8   gadget, invention, solution, machine, piece of equipment, technique
     9   sample, selection, shot
   10   attempt, effort, result, answer, safety measure, protection
   11   act, decision, course of action
   12   move, decision, course of action, answer, person

Revision exercises

R1   1 results in not taking action, even when necessary
        2 has a high probability of being dangerous
        3 it is bad to think too well of yourself
        4 makes something less than perfect
        5 can be uncomfortable, or even dangerous
        6 it is bad to throw anything away which could be useful, also sometimes wastes are in themselves dangerous
        7 being rude to sb never helps a situation
        8 is dangerous to others
        9 causes mental suffering
     10 destroys buildings, crops, sometimes people and animals
     11 usually causes problems or suffering
     12 not having enough to eat causes suffering and maybe even death
     13 cause changes in body chemistry which are usually bad
     14 destroying everything
     15 problems and dangers which are difficult to avoid
     16 a person whose mind is disturbed suffers and causes suffering to others
     17 implies preventing from breathing, or growing or functioning properly
     18 it is bad to think too well of yourself, means you do not try to improve

R2   1 lucrative   2 endless   3 incompatible   4 shrewd   5 random
    6 remote   7 synthetic   8 application   9 component   10 float
    11 task   12 ambivalent

R3   1 [+ importance]   2 [+ condition] [+ bad]   3 [+ to be noticed]
    4 [+ guided by one's sense of what is right]   5 [+ hairs]   6 [+ meet]
    [+ accidentally]   7 [+ dirt covering surface]

R4   see Student's Book, grid 5, p 10

R5   1 see Student's Book, grid 3, p 13
    2 see Student's Book, grid 6, p 28

R6   1 value   2 assessed   3 handsome   4 charming   5 chores   6 task
    7 conceit   8 filthy   9 conscientious   10 carefree   11 careful
    12 remote

R7   1 injured   2 impaired   3 damaged   4 harmed   5 ruined
    6 muttered   7 scruffy   8 filthy   9 powerful   10 assessing   11 strong   12 potent   13 dissecting   14 superseded
    15 unsightly   16 scope   17 range   18 estimating   19 reckless
    20 calamity   21 forestall   22 effective

Unit 3

1   1 a piece of rope, cord, string   2 a sole and leather or cloth   3 a drill or a sharp instrument   4 cloth, buttons, thread, a sewing machine
    5 twigs, feathers, straw   6 wood, slate, straw, tiles   7 leather, plastic
    8 wood and wire

2   1 error   2 rising, setting, morning   3 knot   4 role, part   5 attain
6 same   7 neck, legs   8 end   9 price   10 mere   11 wear
12 effort, pains

3   1 [+ poor quality] [+ dry]   2 [+ watchful]   3 [+ harmful]
4 [+ dull] [+ gloomy]   5 [+ sorrowful]   6 [+ poor quality]
7 [+ honest] [+ true]   8 [+ useful]   9 [+ charming]   10 [+ strict]
[+ firm]   11 [+ enormous]   12 [+ direct refusal]   13 [+ beast of
prey] [+ kills and eats others]

4   1 crutches   2 pebbles   3 hierarchy   4 artifact   5 fur   6 spurn
7 yearning   8 weave   9 bees   10 sever

5   1 paper, regular, intricate, complicated   2 fine, fashion, impressive
3 tremendous, impressive, great   4 arid, fertile, rich, dry, wet   5 hexagonal, rectangular, irregular   6 humiliating, pleasant, good   7 rapid,
slow, deliberate, graceful   8 deafening, enormous, damaging

6   1   to reply to an attack with similar action or speech
    2   to send out a bright, cold light or flashes of brilliant light
    3   to press together or on with force so as to break, injure or spoil
    4   to produce offspring
    5   to allow to run over or fall out
    6   (of animals or human beings) to kill in large numbers
    7   to travel through little-known parts (of land or sea) in order to learn
      more
    8   to pass from one side to the other
    9   to wonder greatly, to be surprised
   10   to strike with the beak

7   1 cloth, piece of work, gadget, machine   2 person, cook, housekeeper,
worker   3 health, problem, colour, person, flower   4 day, season, afternoon, climate   5 nature, movement, touch   6 housewife, business man,
mother   7 animal, bird, fish, dolphin   8 approach, regime, object,
design   9 feelings, sympathy, interest, antique, letter   10 construction,
bar, pole, wall   11 line, wall, road, row, pole   12 note, tone, voice,
cry, demand   13 care, enquiry, concern   14 person, organisation,
revolt, movement, activist

8   1 deep, deeply   2 delicate   3 affectionate   4 separate   5 torrential
6 vigorous   7 repetitious   8 touching, touchy   9 rigid   10 comfortable   11 proud   12 extinct

9   1 the earth quakes; a person quakes or quivers (with cold, for example)
    2 to reach a place; to attain one's object
    3 to scrutinize is to examine with great thoroughness; to inspect is to
      examine carefully and closely, (often) officially
    4 to refuse is to say no to something, to show unwillingness to give or
      accept something; to reject is not to accept an offer or a fact
    5 to glance is to take a quick look
    6 to squat is to sit on the heels

10   1 chase   2 lounged   3 struggled   4 anticipate   5 link   6 paced
7 begged   8 gentle   9 shed   10 awake

11   1 **to whisper** is to speak in a low, soft voice, or under the breath; **to talk**
    is to speak

2 **to glow** is to give off heat or light without flame; **to glitter** is to send out bright, cold light or flashes of brilliant light

3 **to cry** is to call loudly, to make a loud sound especially a sound that expresses feelings (eg pain, fear); **to shout** is to speak in a loud voice, to make a loud cry

4 **to fight** is any kind of aggression between animals or people; **to struggle** suggests physical combat between two individuals, or aggression between a minority and a majority

5 **to tear** is to pull apart by force; **to destroy** is to break to pieces

6 **to fly** is to move through the air

7 **mature** is ripe, or full-grown, fully developed; **old** is near the end of its life

8 **infantile** is childish, not mature; **young** is not old

9 **sensuous** is appealing to the human senses, eg sensuous music; **sensitive** is quick to receive impressions

10 **a bond** is a written agreement or promise, usually about money; **a knot** is a fastening in rope, cord, or string

11 **arid soil** is generally dry in character and not good for growing things; **dry soil** is not necessarily arid, and may be temporarily dry

12
1 coverings that grow from a bird's skin
2 small, round, juicy fruits with many small seeds
3 the overhanging edges of a roof
4 garden behind a house
5 residential area on the outside of a city
6 *of* small building in a garden, for pleasure
7 fanatics, people having strong unchanging belief in sth
8 the hard, horny part of a bird's mouth
9 where the bird lays its eggs
10 a lid or cover of a bottle
11 dry, arid area of land
12 sticks to help an injured person to walk

13
1 banned   2 pleasant   3 ruptured   4 longed for   5 victory
6 solicitous   7 diminishing   8 challenge

14
1 similar   both are collections of individuals
  different   a **society** is a large group organised according to mutually agreed rules and conventions
2 similar   both concern a ranking of individual items or people in order of importance or dominance
  different   **pecking order** concerns chickens, but may apply to other animals or people by extension
3 similar   both mean to come in
  different   **to slip into** implies doing so quietly and without causing disturbance
4 similar   both concern looking at sth
  different   **scrutinize** is to examine very carefully
5 similar   in both cases the object breaks
  different   **crush** is to apply steady pressure until the object breaks; **crash** is to suddenly come into contact with an object
6 similar   results in death
  different   **slaughter** is for animals, or if used for humans, means large numbers die, often in a cruel way

7 similar   both are cleaning
  different   **grooming** is done to animals with fur, either by other animals, or by humans; **groom** is also used for women

8 similar   both mean removing sth which is not one's own
  different   **steal** is take with the intention of not returning

9 similar   to follow sth or sb to catch it
  different   **chase** is follow behind at a speed similar to the thing pursued, whereas **hunt** is to use any means to catch

10 similar   both mean depart from somewhere
  different   **bustle off** is to leave in a way which suggests activity, a lot to do, effort

Revision exercises

R1   1 see Student's Book, grid 2, p 25
    2 see Student's Book, grid 2, p 7

R2   1 [+ pride in oneself] [+ over-high]   2 [+ misfortune] [+ widespread]
    3 [+ dirt] [+ causing disgust]   4 [+ pride in oneself] [+ justified]
    5 [+ move] [+ from side to side] 6 [+ future event]
    [+ tell]   7 [+ place on a numerical scale]

R3   1 assessment, assessor 2 prophet, prophecy 3 rating, rate
    4 response 5 fertilizer, fertility 6 application, applicant 7 exposure
    8 perception 9 destruction 10 prediction 11 finding, finder
    12 inference 13 estimate, estimation 14 solution 15 assumption
    16 acknowledgement

R4   1 flourishing 2 legislation 3 scruffy 4 trampled 5 wig 6 confident 7 spilled 8 satellite 9 harness 10 deposits

R5   1 [+ take the place of because better]   2 [+ examine] [+ superficially]
    3 [+ say no] [+ politely]   4 [+ succeed in completing]   5 [+ tremble]
    [+ from cold]   6 [+ look] [+ intently]   7 [+ look] [+ as in wonder]
    8 [+ want to fight] [+ for a cause]   9 [+ return the same sort of treatment]   10 [+ cannot be understood]   11 [+ be present in large numbers]   12 [+ short period of rest]   13 [+ underground channel]
    [+ carries off waste]   14 [+ object to be aimed at]

R6   1 they all mean to count up the worth of, but whereas **assess** implies precise analysis, **value** implies positive judgement, and **rate** implies numerical scale
    2 they all denote a form of damaging, but whereas **injure** causes wounds, **impair** makes worse in function, and **mar** makes an abstract object less than perfect
    3 they all denote arriving at an opinion about sth, but whereas **judge** means to form an opinion about, **conclude** and **infer** both mean to arrive at an opinion by reasoning
    4 both **generate** and **produce** mean bring into existence, cause to be, but **generate** is only used with a few nouns (see grid)
    5 plight is a bad condition
    6 both **effective** and **efficacious** mean capable of bringing about definite results, but **efficacious** implies beneficial, good results

R7   1 to rate, estimate, assess something at
    2 to conclude, infer from something that

     3 to inspect, examine, check, scan, scrutinize something for
     4 to shake, tremble, quiver, shiver, shudder with

R8
   1 rubbish, water, waste, rubble, stones, wood
   2 a project, plan, idea, course of action, person, child, animal, hope
   3 a competitor, challenge, attempt to do sth, a person
   4 acts, ideas, opinions, social rules, behaviour, attitudes
   5 difficulties, problems
   6 illnesses, physical weakness, a hot climate, a cold climate
   7 a carpet, branch, umbrella, one's fist, sb's opinion, belief
   8 sb's health, sb's happiness, sb's whereabouts, sth one wants to buy, a
      service, trains, planes, ships, departure times
   9 the weather, the economic situation, the state of currency, sb's
      success
  10 sb's income, damages, the value of sth
  11 a problem, an analysis, a description, a situation, a schema, an explan-
      ation
  12 sb's movements, sb's vision, individual freedom
  13 gifts, letters, receipt of letters/parcels/books, a person's presence
  14 a holiday, a stay in England, good advice

R9   1 a dog of no special breed or of mixed breed   2 place where trials and
judicial activities take place   3 a market where stocks and shares are sold
and bought   4 to cut sth which grows, eg a hedge, one's nails   5 to
cause, be the start of   6 to draw out   7 to prove to be untrue or false
8 to speak in a low indistinct voice, to murmur, to grumble   9 merciless,
without pity   10 likely to be a direct cause of cancer   11 selected
without criteria   12 contradictory in appearance, attitude or status

R10   1 house, window, clothes, face   2 worker, secretary, piece of work
3 view, music, resemblance, cousin   4 spender, adventurer, driver
5 bad weather, a bad harvest, unemployment   6 sb's action, a surpise
attack, sb's intention   7 sb's ability, property, advice

R11   1 warned   2 irrigated   3 devastated   4 anticipated   5 relevance
         6 pitfalls   7 forestalled   8 overt   9 profitable   10 scope

R12

Unit 4

1   1 it failed to have its intended effect   2 play according to the rules, to do as it should be done   3 the product was a big success   4 what you are saying is so hard to believe that I think you are not serious   5 what is the last line (of story or joke) which makes the point of the whole thing?
6 the advertisement (commercial) was broadcast on television or radio
7 try to take advantage of sth   8 that's exaggerated   9 we had to go back to, to rely on this method (which we used before)

2   1 to make a product or service known to the public   2 a hoarding is put up for displaying advertisements of goods   3 babies wear them before they learn how to use a lavatory   4 a cream to keep the skin healthy
5 to darken the eyelashes and make them look longer   6 to make the eyes more beautiful   7 to put a glossy coating on the nails   8 small model imitating a person or animal, used in dramatic presentation

3   1 large, huge   2 soft   3 dry   4 speed up   5 marked, important, large
6 scarcity, lack, shortage, insufficiency   7 fall asleep   8 costly, expensive   9 inferior   10 irresponsible

4   1 news, paper, bath   2 scene, woman, speech   3 attempt, insult, lie
4 measure, remedy, order   5 child, birth, purpose, reason   6 detail, theory, person   7 merchandise, goods, work   8 meal, housekeeper, life
9 picture, scene, imagination   10 accident, show, scene   11 wine, eyes, diamonds   12 drugs, conversation, atmosphere, person

5   1 salvation, saving(s)   2 constraint   3 preference   4 condition, conditioning   5 promotion, promoter   6 abundance   7 resistance
8 truth   9 wisdom   10 scarcity

6   1 **to follow** is to come or go after (in order, space or time), whereas **to haunt** is to keep coming back to the mind or to appear repeatedly in (especially of ghosts)
    2 both denote making a journey on foot, but **to roam** is to wander, to walk here and there without any particular destination
    3 both denote a change of position, but **to flop down** means to fall down in a clumsy, helpless way
    4 both denote a change of state, but whereas **to wake up** means to stop sleeping, to become conscious, **to get up** means to rise, to get out of bed
    5 both mean to increase, but **to mark up goods** means to put a higher price on them, and **to raise prices** is to increase prices generally
    6 both use goods, but **a consumer** is more particularly a person who buys the goods that he will use himself (the contrary of producer)
    7 both are social classes, but whereas the working class consists of those members of society who work with their hands, the middle class is the part of society between the working class and the aristocracy
    8 both are devices to make goods known to people, but whereas an ad is a notice in a newspaper about things to be sold or things that are needed, a poster is a bill or a placard on which something is announced or advertised
    9 both mean poor, but whereas **meagre** is unsatisfactory (eg a meagre meal), **scanty** means not so much as is needed
   10 **straight** meaning by a direct route, without delay, is the opposite of **indirect**

7 1 tell 2 tears 3 bet 4 grow, become, get 5 range 6 buy
7 take up 8 acquired 9 matter 10 most

8 1 vivid 2 pursuit 3 simple 4 immune 5 commodities 6 goods
7 stand 8 frugal 9 plain 10 amazed

9 1 embody 2 receive 3 respond 4 frighten 5 persuade 6 invest
7 dry 8 use 9 wrap 10 devise

10 1 rubber, sugar, fibre, copper, iron ore 2 washing machines, record
players, cars, cameras 3 gloves, handbags, suitcases, shoes 4 tools,
nails, screws, locks, keys, paint, wood 5 knives, forks, teapots, jugs,
cups, trays 6 hammers, nails, saws, scissors

11 1 elegant, awkward, primitive 2 soft, smooth, fair, thick, thin, dark,
black, brown 3 good, new, well-known 4 fine, applied, romantic,
classical 5 glossy, clear, bright red 6 pleasant, trying, interesting,
unusual 7 slow, speedy, quick, miraculous 8 fascinating, captivating,
dull, funny, sad, appealing, long, short 9 amusing, unfair, cunning,
clever 10 quick, slow, predictable, likely, unlikely, personal

12 1 similar   both express happiness with facial expression
     different   **laugh** includes noise as well
  2 similar   both mean react to a definite stimulus from sb or sth else
     different   **answer** is only verbal activity in response to a question
       respond also means to react to a stimulus
  3 similar   enclose goods for safety or convenience
     different   **wrap**, only by putting sth flat (eg paper) around the outside
  4 similar   both facial expressions
     different   **grin** is a wide smile expression pleasure, **smirk** may be un-
       pleasant
  5 similar   both ways of laughing
     different   **giggle** is to laugh in a nervous way, whereas **chuckle** is to
       laugh with a low-pitched sound as if to oneself
  6 similar   all structures in the street from which things are sold
     different   **kiosks** are for newspapers and sweets, **stalls** and **stands** are
       usually movable and temporary
  7 similar   both are flat pieces of wood
     different   a **shelf** is fixed, for storing things
  8 similar   both used by advertisers to sell goods
     different   a **trick** deceives, a **gimmick** makes people notice sth in a
       special way
  9 similar   both are bought
     different   a **bargain** is bought at less than the normal price
  10 similar   both involve beginning
     different   **onset** is of sth bad
  11 similar   both refer to quantities
     different   **scant** is just sufficient, whereas **scanty** is inadequate
  12 similar   both imply richness, wealth
     different   **affluent** implies having almost everything one wants,
       whereas **opulent** suggests deliberately displaying that one
       has wealth
  13 similar   both connected with large size
     different   **huge** implies on a large scale, enormous, impressive

14 similar   refers to quantities, usually of food
different   **scanty** means inadequate, **frugal** implies the minimum necessary for survival

13   1 trick   2 austere   3 affluent   4 opulent   5 roaming   6 laugh   7 smile   8 nap   9 destiny   10 producer

Revision exercises

R1   1 an attack   2 an offer   3 monotony   4 lack of adaptability, hunting by man   5 free market system   6 efficient work   7 an accident to the legs   8 birds eating   9 not getting enough food or the right sort of food   10 smoke and fog mixing   11 extreme shortage of food   12 radiation, change in diet

R2   1 opulent   2 daily   3 knowledgeable   4 potent   5 responsive   6 factual   7 costly   8 conscious   9 austere   10 infantile   11 analogous   12 linear   13 genetic   14 vain   15 proud   16 touchy, touching   17 hazardous   18 restrictive   19 fertile   20 assertive   21 grimy   22 affluent

R3   1 **check**   see Student's Book, grid 2, p 43
2 **spurn**   see Student's Book, grid 5, p 46

R4   1 marred   2 forecast   3 baffle   4 efficacious   5 glimpsed   6 change   7 lure   8 risky   9 calamity   10 evaluate   11 slipped   12 trotted

R5   **generate** [+ energy, force]
plight [+ bad situation]
infer [+ form an opinion] [+ by imaginative deduction from given information]
conceit [+ exaggerated] [+ good opinion] [+ of oneself or what one has done]
wig [+ covering of hair] [+ artificial]
date [+ appointment] [+ with a member of the opposite sex]
task [+ piece of work] [+ assigned]
grimy [+ dirt covering surface]
rate [+ by placing or as if by placing on a numerical scale]
self-esteem [+ good opinion of oneself or what one has done] [+ justified]
bump into [+ meet] [+ accidentally]

R6   1 sb's action, an attempt   2 the importance of something, sb's ability   3 face, house, clothes   4 sb as a leader, a present, clothes, sb's reputation   5 face, view, flower, house   6 hatred, electricity   7 face, present, man   8 clothes, face   9 lecture, view, dinner party, house, clothes, man, occupation   10 hatred, attempt   11 occupation, proposal   12 sb's reputation, children, one's legs   13 the environment, one's health, sb's reputation,   14 sb's car, a painting, the environment, one's health, sb's reputation   15 children, one's legs, sb's feelings, sb's pride

R7   1 efficient   2 distant   3 valid   4 relevant   5 flourishing   6 gauge   7 random   8 gazed   9 destructive   10 trampled   11 worsened   12 devastating

R8   1 silts   2 complacency   3 nuclear fission   4 liability   5 infest   6 incompatible   7 peer   8 proliferation   9 inherent   10 euphoria   11 detergent   12 squat

R9 1 reach 2 gained 3 distant 4 achieved 5 accomplish 6 attaining 7 harmful 8 pernicious 9 shoddy 10 squatted 11 ruffled 12 plaintive 13 shuddered 14 shiver 15 retaliate 16 sever 17 shake 18 shakes 19 quake 20 peered 21 glimpsed 22 antics 23 munched 24 spurning 25 scanned 26 scrutinizing 27 examine 28 check 29 reject 30 turned down

Unit 5

1 1 level of awareness of life attained by adults 2 infantilism is being like a child and adulticism is being like an adult 3 a boyfriend you go out with regularly 4 either father alone or mother alone 5 buying sth by paying a sum of money each month 6 get on well 7 her child, now a 32-year-old adult, appeared at her house 8 they think feeling satisfied with what one achieves is more important than being rich 9 a prediction which is hard to believe, and not good 10 don't be afraid to discipline your children

2 1 a child, a wife or husband, a dog, a girlfriend, boyfriend
2 a club, society, university, political group, generation
3 a crime, a fire, an accident, dangerous driving, social changes
4 your will, a regime, heavy taxation, restrictions on imports, duty on cigarettes, yourself on sb
5 a door, a car-door, a window, a book on a table, a drawer
6 tensions, a bad atmosphere, problems
7 trouble, problems, tension, disagreement, arguments, dissention
8 enquiries, demands, requests, intolerant people
9 an offer, your services, your labour, your help
10 a target, an improvement, a certain level of knowledge, a time of arrival
11 a friend, a politician, a business man, a company
12 the law, the rules, your parents, the captain of a ship, an officer in the army
13 money, social behaviour, domestic problems
14 a problem, a difficulty, a situation, a job, an exam paper
15 the right to do sth, an inheritance, a tax rebate, a prize, a reward
16 an opinion, a point of view, good relations
17 a bar, a pub, a restaurant, a night club, a casino
18 your life style, your attitude, your behaviour, your method of doing sth

3 1 offspring, young 2 menace 3 outcome, upshot 4 adult 5 shift 6 maintain 7 to lose one's temper 8 abandon 9 complain 10 grant 11 cajole 12 tidy

4 1 with 2 on 3 up, aside 4 to 5 to 6 about 7 about, over 8 with 9 at 10 on

5 1 similar   telling something
different **overstate** is exaggerate
2 similar   to have a good relationship with sb
different **like** is definitely want to be with sb

3 similar to move out of the way of an object
  different **dodge** is a sudden sideways movement
4 similar looking for sth
  different **trace back** is systematically follow a series of events back
  through time
5 similar to strike another person
  different **kick** is only with the leg
6 similar coming to a place, event
  different **show up** is colloquial
7 similar both mean not fat in physical appearance
  different **skinny** is so thin as to be unattractive
8 similar having good manners
  different **courteous** implies following traditional rules of
  politeness
9 similar having an able, quick mind
  different **crafty** means also able to and likely to deceive others for
  gain
10 similar all are printed paper publications
  different **newspapers** have only paper pages and are not usually
  coloured, they appear daily, or weekly; **newsletters** are
  usually produced privately for example by a club or society
  or company, and have a small circulation; **magazines**
  usually have coloured card covers, contain many pictures,
  and appear weekly or monthly

6 1 similar quick witted
  different **sly** is skillful in deceiving, whereas **shrewd** is able to make
  good judgements of situations and people
2 similar neat arrangement, good appearance
  different **orderly** also implies a reasoned arrangement according to a
  classification
3 similar lack of certainty
  different **dubious** may suggest suspicious, or dishonest or bad
4 similar not imposing rules or discipline
  different **lenient** is doing so kindly and reasonably, **permissive** is too
  lenient
5 similar both are pieces of work
  different a **chore** is a dull routine piece of work which you don't like
  doing
6 similar to quarrel about small unimportant things
  different very close in meaning, but **squabble** suggests childishness
7 similar to take care of young
  different **rear** for animals, **bring up** for children
8 similar to go to
  different **to attend** for meetings, lectures, courses, classes, clinics; **to
  frequent** for bars, restaurants, clubs, regularly
9 similar complaining
  different **bellyache** is slang, **grumble** is complain by talking about sth
  a lot, but not doing anything to try to change it
10 similar complaining by one person to another on a personal level
  different **nag** implies unpleasantly and for too long

7 1 from 2 with 3 up 4 from, against 5 about, at 6 on 7 to,
about 8 with 9 to 10 for

8   cunning: smile, person, trick
orderly: person, progress, queue of people, garden
lenient: judge, laws, person, disposition
tidy: person, garden, clothes, handwriting
shrewd: judge, smile, person, judge of character, trick, politician
neat: person, garden, clothes, handwriting
sly: disposition, smile, person
permissive: laws, morals, society
steady: pace, boyfriend, progress, person
crafty: smile, person, trick, politician
even: pace, disposition

9   1 informal, colloquial   2 colloquial   3 formal   4 colloquial
5 informal, colloquial   6 formal, informal, colloquial   7 colloquial
8 colloquial   9 colloquial   10 informal, colloquial   11 informal,
colloquial   12 informal, colloquial

10   1 grow   2 gentle   3 permissive   4 option   5 findings   6 sacrifice
7 protected   8 breed   9 claimed   10 traced

11   1 grow   2 restricted   3 confined   4 lenient   5 crafty   6 shrewd
7 cope with   8 grumbled   9 moan   10 adult

Revision exercises

R1   1 one behind the other, making one line only   2 for several minutes, continuously, without interruption   3 escape, get free   4 house not owned by people who live in it, owned by the administrative council of the town or region   5 suspect, with little evidence   6 abnormal member of a species, result of change in structre of genes   7 to look at him just when he happens to be looking at you   8 other effects than those intended, usually bad   9 main constituent of exhaust from cars   10 work continuously, without a rest   11 (for monkeys, apes and humans) with all four limbs on the ground   12 a falling behind in time in food production   13 have a serious disagreement, difficult to resolve

R2   1 good

			bad
self-esteem	pride	vanity	conceit

2 not very

		very
dirty	grimy grubby	filthy

3 least

				greatest
surprise	astonish	amaze	astound	flabbergast

4 slightly disturbing

					very disturbing
tease **bother**	pester	nag get on at	worry	plague	harass harry

R3   hardware, silverware, glassware, ironware, stoneware, houseware, kitchenware; household goods, consumer goods, leather goods, perishable goods, dry goods, luxury goods

R4   1 [+ return] [+ the same sort of ill treatment]   2 [+ grotesque] 3 [+ sit] [+ on the heels, with the knees bent]   4 [+ mislead] [+ by presenting false information]   5 [+ look at, over] [+ usu closely, carefully] [+ in order to detect errors]   6 [+ make impure or poisonous] [+ by contact with harmful matter]   7 [+ not worrying about possible consequences]   8 [+ dry] [+ often without life]   9 [+ contemptuously] 10 [+ shake] [+ often because of fear]   11 [+ reach] [+ usu of sth above average]

R5   1 bottle tops 2 eyelashes, eyebrows, eyeshadow, eye play 3 household goods, household commodities, household duties, household chores 4 leather goods 5 consumer goods, consumer society 6 flashcard, flashlight 7 court settlements 8 lipstick 9 pitfall 10 paper and pencil measures 11 side effects 12 weather forecast, weather report 13 brain cells 14 insurance company 15 stock market 16 crutchwords 17 application form 18 city dweller 19 nail polish, nail varnish 20 life style 21 skin conditioner 22 doorsteps

R6   self-esteem, self-confident, self-conscious, self-confidence, self-possessed, self-display, self-fulfilment, self-oriented, self-respect (in the texts); a selection of others: self-control, self-defence, self-evident, self-expression, self-government, self-sacrifice, self-supporting, self-restraint, self-righteous, self-knowledge, self-effacing

R7   1 grooming 2 ruffled 3 quaked 4 prey 5 rank 6 anxious 7 scanned 8 scrutinized 9 fastidious 10 alert

R8   1 primates 2 crutches 3 predators 4 arbour 5 artifact 6 eaves 7 slippers 8 troops 9 feat 10 rupture 11 scurry 12 mate 13 smart

R9   1 see Student's Book, grid 3, p 68
2 see Student's Book, grid 7, p 67
3 see Student's Book, grid 3, p 64

R10   1 hazardous 2 foresee 3 powerful 4 deteriorate 5 tempted 6 alter 7 glanced 8 assessed 9 blooming 10 retaliated 11 warned 12 attaining, gaining

R11   1 belief 2 behaviour(ist) 3 awareness 4 courtesy 5 strength 6 victim, victimization 7 authorization 8 giant 9 hero, heroine, heroism, 10 environment 11 pride 12 vanity

R12   1 primary school 2 block of flats 3 telephone kiosk, telephone box 4 chemist's 5 hoarding 6 rubbish 7 nappy 8 petrol 9 angry, cross 10 to post

R13   see Student's Book, grid 5, p 66

R14

Unit 6

1   1 who has taken a degree in a university and is studying for a higher
     degree   2 one who is associated with another in duty or occupation
     3 a man who is in charge of a group of workmen   4 a person who has
     special knowledge, skill, or practice   5 one who asks for or tries to get a
     job or a place on a course   6 a person who takes care of a house or
     building, who keeps it clean   7 a person who calculates risks to make
     insurance policies more accurate   8 a regular payment to a person who
     has ceased active work   9 an arrangement to meet someone at a fixed
     time and place   10 a place where ships are built or repaired   11 the
     secret damaging of the enemy's property   12 a period of free time for
     rest and special study (given to university teachers in Great Britain)

2   1 managerial   2 provocative   3 continuous, continual   4 attractive
     5 lively   6 glamorous   7 vocational   8 skilled, skillful   9 formal
     10 diversified   11 personal, personable   12 quarrelsome   13 clerical
     14 profitable   15 occupational   16 axiomatic   17 imaginary
     18 deadly, dead   19 spectacular   20 fictional

3   1 answer, response, gesture, remark, letter, course of action
     2 meeting, party, gathering, dinner, lunch, dress, outfit, approach
     3 work, duties, post, skills
     4 work, workman, craftsman, operator, job
     5 industry, advance, step forward, factor, consideration
     6 formula, key, spell, circle, wand

7 industry, nation, trend, problem, tendency
8 undertaking, enterprise, venture, association, meeting, deal
9 job, life, life-style, girl, clothes
10 interest
11 news, invention, discovery, find, development
12 results, discovery, find, development, event, explosion, procession, display

4 1 for 2 over to 3 of 4 on 5 to 6 on 7 to 8 with 9 out
10 of 11 with, against 12 for, against, with

5 1 reply 2 part 3 dullness 4 reason(ing) 5 schedule 6 inferiors
7 penalty 8 delete, omit 9 assess 10 get to know, familiarize oneself with 11 be naked 12 resign, abandon 13 delay, put off
14 leave 15 keep in mind

6 1 similar   both concern work
   different **grind** is tedious, long, routine work which you don't like **labour** is often physical work
2 similar   both are people who like you
   different **fans** like and support your professional work, **friends** are more personal
3 similar   both ask for information
   different **query** refers to questions, usu short, about recently given information; a **question** may be on a completely new topic
4 similar   both are lawyers
   different **barristers** only work in courts of law, **solicitors** give general legal advice
5 similar   both refer to work
   different **drudgery** is non-creative, tedious work, whereas **toil** is long and tiring, usually physical work
6 similar   refer to animate being's physical state
   different **alive** is simply not dead, whereas **lively** is active, moving about a lot
7 similar   both mean that the thing concerned is not real or genuine
   different **mock** is in close imitation of sth, and intended as a substitute for it, eg mock cream, whereas **sham** suggests the speaker does not like the imitation and that it is in bad taste
8 similar   both concern receiving sth in return for a service
   different **unrewarding** refers to work from which one does not derive any pleasure and in which one does not make much progress; **unrewarded** refers to a person who does not receive anything in return for service done
9 similar   both mean that the thing concerned is not real or genuine
   different **bogus** implies also that the speaker finds the imitation in bad taste
10 similar both mean to take sth away from sth else
   different **divest** has a very limited use, collocating only with clothes, and distinctions, privileges or power
11 similar both concern calling to mind sth one needs to think of
   different **remember** is to call to mind oneself, **remind** is to cause sb else to do so

12 similar   not knowing what to do or say
    different **be stumped for** is colloquial and applies particularly to answers to questions, or solutions to problems
13 similar   both mean avoiding sth one should do
    different **evade** is avoid by quick-wittedness or deception, **shirk** is avoid because of laziness or cowardice

7   1 a position in a foreign country   2 the difference in value between a country's exports and imports   3 a short phase designed to make people remember the name of a product   4 not real cream   5 copy typist who works with a group of other typists under supervision   6 false document stating that one is qualified as a doctor   7 additional benefits to a job apart from wages or salary   8 illness linked to a certain occupation or work   9 ticket (provided by employer) which is exchanged for lunch by employee   10 interest for reasons of personal gain or security   11 skills required of a clerk or office worker   12 football played by professional players, not amateurs   13 the price of tickets for going and returning   14 making a fine show   15 turn away one's eyes   16 *lit* a carved pole having magical or religious significance to a group of people (usu primitive)

8   1 **dodge**   see Student's Book, grid 3, p 105
    2 **strip**   see Student's Book, grid 4, p 106

9   1 take on   2 ad   3 demand   4 vocational   5 stumped   6 field
    7 supply   8 keep, on

10   1 similar   money paid in return for regular work
    different a **salary** is monthly paid, usu by cheque, whereas **wages** are weekly paid, usu in cash, for manual or clerical work
    2 similar   both refer to one's job
    different **occupation** is a general term, **profession** applies only to certain occupations requiring higher education and special training, eg law, medicine
    3 similar   both are not pleasing to the senses
    different **drab** is only for things one sees, and suggests dark in colour, and cheerless; **dull** suggests uninteresting and monotonous
    4 similar   paying careful attention to detail
    different **fastidious** is setting a high standard of perfection, whereas **fussy** is giving too much importance to minor details
    5 similar   made to imitate sth else
    different **counterfeit** is intended to deceive for gain, and is used of money and documents; **phony** is colloquial and suggests that the object arouses suspicion
    6 similar   to cause sth to become different
    different **amend** is make changes to sth written or drawn, in order to improve it
    7 similar   to bring sth or sb back to a former condition
    different **revive** is only bring back to life
    8 similar   to avoid undesirable things or events
    different **ward off** is keep undesirable things at a distance, eg disease, intruders, whereas **avert** is stop undesirable events from happening

11   see Student's Book, grid 6, p 108

12   1 improved   2 punishment   3 wry   4 false   5 shifted   6 deadly
7 fussy   8 acquired   9 merit   10 occupation

Revision exercises

R1   1 babies' nappies which are used once and thrown away   2 advertisements (on radio and TV)   3 pieces of paper or cardboard, fastened to an
object, saying what it is, where it is to go, etc   4 paper to wrap up things
with   5 the best   6 reduced price   7 the last line of a joke or story,
which makes the point of the whole thing   8 be safe, secure, protected
from   9 put a lower price on it   10 return, rely on   11 defy, resist,
openly disobey   12 one after the other   13 like sb and enjoy their
company   14 in the same way, for the same reasons   15 scatter, drive
away all doubts   16 make clear, explain

R2   1 anything one is dissatisfied with   2 a disagreement   3 sb does sth
funny, or unusual, or they are too proud   4 objection to violence and
war   5 information on the victim which the latter does not want to be
made public   6 anger   7 fear and uncertainty   8 dislike sb, have a
grudge against them   9 feeling frustrated and dissatisfied, being a perfec-
tionist   10 anything too difficult to understand   11 unkind amusement
at sb else's misfortune   12 wanting to hide, avoid being seen, avoid being
hit, avoid wind or snow or rain   13 something very amazing   14 fear or
disgust   15 suspicion that something is wrong   16 being dissatisfied
17 pain, sorrow, dissatisfaction

R3   1 at   2 at   3 into, out   4 off   5 to   6 to   7 from, to   8 from
9 with   10 from

R4   1 argue   2 theorize   3 describe   4 maintain   5 threaten   6 entail
7 oblige   8 bury   9 abound   10 consume   11 perceive   12 respond   13 suspect   14 proliferate

R5   1 tore   2 achieve   3 aim, ambition   4 prey   5 dodged   6 amended
7 restore   8 complained   9 toil   10 temper   11 perilous

R6   1 standby   2 cereal   3 hoarding   4 gimmicks   5 monks
6 heir, heiress   7 opulent   8 grin

R7   1 discontent, belief, flooding, habit   2 transition, increase, decrease,
change, improvement   3 situation, state, person, loan, investment
4 bag, sack, load, burden, suitcase   5 behaviour, attitude, idea, smile,
language   6 boyfriend, speed, progress, deterioration, improvement, job
7 politician, fox, move, person   8 attitude, person, childhood, school,
atmosphere

R8   scan [+ to look at (over)] [+ usually quickly, superficially]
accomplish [+ success in completing task]
foretell [+ tell of some future event] [+ without a sound factual basis]
mar [+ with abstract objects] [+ make less than perfect]
overt [+ open] [+ of actions, attitudes] [+ to be noticed]
mutter [+ in a low voice] [+ indistinctly] [+ speak]
devastate [+ leave nothing that can be used]
hazardous [+ dangerous]
lucrative [+ bringing a lot of money]
assess [+ count up the worth of] [+ implies precise analysis]

cower [+ lower oneself with the legs drawn up under the body] [+ in great fear]
baffle [+ confuse] [+ make extremely difficult to understand]

R9   1 reach   2 bluffed   3 deceived   4 victim   5 glowing   6 militant   7 disturbing   8 keep clean   9 eager   10 threaten   11 bustled off   12 eat

R10   1 cues   2 grime   3 mongrel   4 target   5 finding   6 self-esteem   7 ambivalent   8 dissect   9 bump into   10 supersede

R11   1 **reach**   see Student's Book, grid 1, p 43
       2 **shake**   see Student's Book, grid 3, p 26
       3 **distant**   see Student's Book, grid 9, p 30

R12   1 similar   limit sth/sb
         different   **confine** is keep within a certain area, **constrict** is make smaller, tighter or narrower
       2 similar   aggressive behaviour
         different   **tackle** is, literally, take the ball from an opponent in a game, whereas **attack** is begin to fight
       3 similar   both cause a nuisance to sb
         different   **tease** is to laugh at sb, **pester** is to keep asking them questions
       4 similar   complain
         different   **grumble** is complain at length and repeatedly of something, **grouse** is complain without being definite about the subject
       5 similar   connected with continuation of species of life by making new individuals
         different   **breed** is cause new individuals to come into existence; **grow** is either make progress towards adult status, or (of plants) cause to make progress towards adult status
       6 similar   both make a statement
         different   **claim** is assert that sth is true, and try to make others believe it
       7 similar   subject obtains sth he didn't have before
         different   with **welcome**, he is glad to have it
       8 similar   to require sth of sb else
         different   **beg** implies an urgent need, perhaps the difference between life and death
       9 similar   indicate dissatisfaction, sorrow
         different   **moan** is low-pitched sound, **whine** is higher pitched; **moan** is only of humans; by extension, **moan** is complain at length, and unnecessarily; **whine** is complain childishly, in a high-pitched voice
     10 similar   disturb sb
         different   **plague** is for things or people which repeatedly cause a nuisance; **harass** has only human subjects and is deliberate
     11 similar   to go away from the place where one is
         different   **run away** is leave a place where one is supposed to be, without permission

12 similar   become parent
   different   **to adopt a child** is to take over (legally) as parents of
   a child born of other parents

R13 1 gaze, glance, glimpse, peer 2 giggle, chuckle 3 grin, smirk
4 dodge, duck, evade, shirk 5 bicker, squabble, wrangle 6 drudgery,
grind, labour, toil, task, job, profession

R14 1 gimmicks 2 ludicrous 3 bargains 4 consumer 5 frugal 6 affluent 7 grocer 8 mark down 9 surprise 10 admit 11 tricks
12 legitimate 13 alarm 14 pursuit 15 nappies 16 disposable
17 amazes 18 consumer 19 puppets 20 manipulated 21 costly
22 drastic 23 roamed 24 austere 25 opulent 26 immune
27 outset 28 outburst 29 astound 30 flabbergasted 31 hunted
32 slice 33 panicking 34 promote 35 hunted

R15

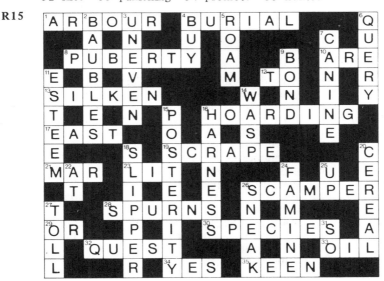

Unit 7

1 1 a clear, open space in a forest 2 a word or phrase used to mean or
describe sth quite different from what it usually expresses 3 a person
who relies on sb else for money to live 4 a person who runs away with a
lover to get married 5 a person in his teens, ie the years of one's age from
13 to 19 6 teaching, instruction 7 simple, plain, homelike, causing
one to think of home 8 made to feel separated and different from a
social group 9 a regularly recurring way of behaving 10 antisocial,
usually illegal conduct by young persons 11 books one reads in bed
before going to sleep 12 avoid talking directly about a subject 13 live
in friendship or harmony with sb 14 to support, to keep from falling
15 to have the same opinion as sb else 16 to feel contented with oneself, not have personal conflicts 17 feel so nervous and mentally ill that
one cannot continue to live and work normally 18 madly in love with

2   1 sb's hand, heaven, a bell, alarm button, controls, success
     2 plants, a garden, flowers, pot plants, vegetables, a lawn
     3 a product eg television, radio, stereo, camera, tape-recorder
     4 violence, traditional methods, checking every product by hand (ie instead of with a machine), non-verbal communication
     5 your image of sb, or of yourself; a situation, a problem
     6 doors and windows, a load, a rope, a cargo
     7 the economy, a good harvest, the outcome of an election, the winner of a sports competition
     8 a problem, yourself, a person, sb who is ill
     9 a project, a plan, a survey, research, an investigation
   10 sb's achievements, sb's success, the effect of sth, sb's claims
   11 animals, seals
   12 statistics, facts, sb's behaviour, what sb says
   13 orders, a reward, bank notes, savings-bonds, stamps
   14 a meal, money, winnings, rooms, problems, work

3   1 carry out 2 void 3 get 4 into 5 wedlock 6 introduce
     7 take 8 give 9 of 10 of

4   1 similar   caring attitude towards sb else's misfortune
       different   **sympathy** suggests understanding, **pity** suggests a feeling of sorrow at what has happened
     2 similar   mental attributes
       different   **reason** is the ability to think logically, **brains** is what one thinks with
     3 similar   both communication by speech
       different   **bark** *fig* is to speak sharply and unkindly
     4 similar   to go away from the place where one was
       different   **go out** is used for leaving enclosed places eg rooms, halls, caves, offices
     5 similar   both processes of heating food to make it good to eat
       different   **cook** is the general term for heating raw food, **boil** is to cook in hot water
     6 similar   to separate sth from other things
       different   **insulate** is place physical barriers to separate, eg put padding round a delicate object to insulate it from shocks
     7 similar   make little progress in moving in water or other liquid substance
       different   **wallow** is to roll about and enjoy being in the liquid, **flounder** is to try with awkward movements to move, but not succeed
     8 similar   send out light
       different   **gleam** is send out a dull light; **glisten** is reflect a dull light
     9 similar   good feelings towards sb
       different   **to be fond of** is to know sb for some time and like them whereas **to be in love with** is sexually motivated strong feelings of love
   10 similar   wanting sth very much
       different   **be greedy** is to want to have too much
   11 similar   both are to feel fear
       different   the differences are mainly distributional

    12 similar   legal agreements between persons of different sexes
       different   **to be engaged** is to have promised to marry sb

5   1 report   2 approach   3 attitude, step forward   4 child, scenery
    5 operation, activity   6 person, speed   7 knot, spot   8 town, possi-
    bility   9 person, number   10 manner, glance   11 behaviour   12 action,
    attitude, behaviour   13 pastime, food, singer, actor, colour   14 move-
    ment, glance   15 sorrow, feeling, person   16 cook, dress

6   1 strange   2 genuine   3 silly   4 stealthy   5 mutual   6 healthy
    7 simple   8 marvellous   9 indefinitely   10 a jump   11 preoccu-
    pation   12 marriage   13 to retain   14 to happen   15 to cry   16 to
    restrict oneself

7   1 [+ respect] [+ fear or reverence]   2 [+ sth bought or sold] [+ at a
    price below its real value]   3 [+ firmly] [+ seize with the hand]
    4 [+ responsibility] [+ for a bad action] 5 [+ sensitive, emotional
    reaction] [+ sharing and understanding of the distress or misfortune of
    another] [+ desire to help and spare]   6 [+ device] [+ for
    catching animals]   7 [+ arousing dislike and/or disgust] [+ very irri-
    tating or disturbing]   8 [+ pretty] [+ neat and delicate in appearance
    and taste]   9 [+ wanting to have] [+ too much]   10 [+ warm and
    friendly] [+ simple and unsophisticated]   11 [+ what it appears or
    claims to be] or [+ sincere and honest] or [+ valid]   12 [+ deceitful]
    [+ not open or straightforward]   13 [+ careful] [+ so as not be to seen]
    14 [+ having well proportioned features] [+ making a pleasant impres-
    sion on the senses]   15 [+ to praise oneself] [+ showing too much
    pride and satisfaction] [+ so as to be noticed] [+ often about sth which
    is not true]   16 [+ praise oneself] [+ showing triumph] [+ so as to be
    noticed]   17 [+ to send out an intermittent light] [+ suddenly and
    briefly] [+ very bright light] [+ once or repeatedly]   18 [+ to reflect
    light] [+ from a smooth, reflective surface] [+ of varying intensity]
    [+ often from a large expanse of water]

8   1 satisfy   2 unite   3 retain   4 permit   5 apply   6 be able   7 lose
    8 disapprove   9 enter   10 achieve

9   1 similar   containers for liquids
       different **bowl** is usu round and deep, **cup** has a handle and is for
                  drinking
    2 similar   ideas in the mind
       different **illusion** is a false idea
    3 similar   people one does not know
       different **a foreigner** is sb from another country
    4 similar   connected with legislation
       different **a bill** is a proposal for a law, which is considered by
                  parliament
    5 similar   simple and unsophisticated
       different **homely** suggests comfortable, kind, sympathetic
    6 similar   refer to activities deliberately kept from the knowledge of
                  certain people
       different **secret** may refer to things which are known to no one; **clan-
                  destine** usu refers to activities against usage or authority
    7 similar   refer to good looks
       different **pretty** is used for small, usu feminine looking things or

people; **handsome** stresses good construction, fine bones if of people, usu refers to men
8 similar to continue to have
different **retain** is more formal, and stresses the possibility of losing
9 similar ways of cooking food
different **roast** is cook sth in an oven, **toast** is expose slices of bread to direct heat so as to turn its outside brown
10 similar both refer to act of describing sth
different **boast** is to praise one's own actions to others, **exaggerate** is go beyond the facts in a description of sth
11 similar refer to movement
different **drift** is move without a definite, predetermined direction
12 similar to make known
different **to reveal** is to make known what is secret or hidden

10 see Student's Book, grid 6, p 129

11 1 complete 2 strange, odd, good 3 firm 4 good, generous 5 great 6 real, hard, good 7 great, amazing 8 successful 9 passionate, friendly, affectionate 10 lasting, long-standing 11 good, free, multiple

12 1 sanity 2 variation, variable, variety 3 frequency 4 relation, relationship, relatedness 5 clarity, clarification 6 gentleness, gentleman 7 loss 8 gift 9 height 10 weight 11 choice 12 finding 13 tendency 14 questionnaire

13 1 obnoxious 2 confidential 3 keep 4 retain 5 jump 6 concealed 7 hid 8 sanity 9 uncertainty 10 fear 11 anxiety 12 bolstered

Revision exercises

R1 1 tremble, shiver, shake, quake, shudder 2 crouch, squat 3 damage, harm, hurt, impair, injure, spoil 4 forestall 5 reject, turn down, decline, spurn 6 shine, glow, gleam, shimmer 7 gaze, glance, glimpse, peer 8 bicker, squabble, wrangle 9 reach, gain, accomplish, achieve 10 filthy, grimy, grubby

R2 1 in 2 for 3 off 4 for 5 to, for 6 from 7 into 8 off 9 to 10 for

R3 1 telephone kiosk, telephone box, telephone call 2 fringe benefits 3 return journey, return ticket 4 felt-tip pen 5 five-day week 6 family life, family responsibilities 7 middle age, middle class 8 assembly line 9 workman, work place 10 head office 11 reference number 12 job market 13 status symbol 14 shipyard 15 day-care centre

R4 1 pay rise 2 holiday 3 lift 4 secondary school 5 primary school 6 petrol 7 rubbish 8 telephone kiosk, telephone box 9 block of flats 10 to post

R5 with life lifelong, lifeless, life cycle, lifetime, life insurance, life expectancy, lifeguard, life-span, life-jacket, lifebelt, lifelike
with self selfless, selfish, self-centered, self-confidence, self-oriented, self-control, self-respect, self-possessed, self-fulfilment, self-esteem, self-pity

R6 1 **check** see Student's Book, grid 2, p 43
2 **tidy** see Student's Book, grid 7, p 87

R7 1 deflate 2 loose 3 genuine 4 rough 5 barren 6 complex,
sophisticated 7 setting 8 slim 9 bottom 10 disobey 11 lose
touch with 12 minor

R8 1 similar   keeping within limits
     different   **to limit** is to keep within a certain size or number or area or
           place; **to restrict** is to keep within a certain size or number
           or to prevent from realizing full potential
    2 similar   complaining, expressing discontent
     different   **to bellyache** is to complain, usu without good reason by
           continually repeating the complaint
    3 similar   making grow
     different   **rear** is usu for animals, **breed** is reproduce or cause to
           reproduce, esp by selection of parents; it is often used
           figuratively in the sense of 'cause'
    4 similar   helping to move forward
     different   **to further** stresses the effort involved
    5 similar   being surprised
     different   **to astonish** is to affect with wonder because difficult to
           believe, whereas **to amaze** is to affect with wonder so as to
           cause confusion
    6 similar   quarrelling
     different   **to squabble** is to quarrel over unimportant matters
           unreasonably and childishly, **to wrangle** is to quarrel
           angrily, noisily, and heatedly
    7 similar   disturbing
     different   **to get on at** is to give no peace of mind by making
           demands and requests, **to harry** is to torment by, or as if by,
           chasing and suggests persistence
    8 similar   both suggest buying and selling
     different   **wares** are man-made, small items usu sold by individuals or
           in small shops, **commodities** are raw materials
    9 similar   shops
     different   a **chain-store** is one of many, owned by the same company;
           general stores are usu small and sell a wide range of goods,
           they are often found in villages
  10 similar   being quick-witted, both suggest skill in deceiving
     different   **sly** is having or showing secretive nature, **crafty** is having or
           showing cleverness and often suggests caution and/or
           subtlety

R9 see Student's Book, grid 3, p 109

R10 A   phony, ludicrous, fussy, scruffy, infantile, sly, selfish, greedy, hostile,
      filthy, conceited, underhanded, drab, obnoxious, a grind, to bully, to
      shirk, to brag, to crow, to blackmail, to bellyache, to bicker
    B   all the rest

R11 see Student's Book, grid 5, p 107

R12 1 job 2 profession 3 leave 4 love 5 counterfeit 6 changed
7 work 8 task 9 grown-up 10 lucky 11 astounded 12 glittering

R13 1 **squabble, bicker, wrangle** see grid 5, p 85
2 **smash, shatter, crush, crack, burst, snap, chip** see grid 4, p 45
3 **smart, elegant, well-groomed** see grid 6, p 11
4 **squat, cower, crouch** see grid 3, p 44
5 **lovely, attractive, charming, good-looking, handsome, pretty** see grid 5, p 10
6 **strong, powerful, potent** see grid 6, p 28

R14

Unit 8

1 1 telepathy 2 ward 3 basement 4 clue 5 sense 6 stage
7 harvest 8 meningitis 9 computer 10 ladybird

2 1 prove 2 attention 3 ring 4 pronounce 5 pass 6 second
7 keep 8 off 9 lend

3 1 psychic 2 human 3 innocent 4 transatlantic, supersonic, non-stop 5 familiar, interesting, strange 6 familiar, well-known 7 vain, unsuccessful 8 heavy, light 9 steady 10 special 11 child, cold-blooded 12 unusual, unlikely, amazing, little-understood

4 1 radiate 2 conviction 3 victimize 4 peaceful 5 fearful, fearless
6 proof 7 coherent 8 ambiguous 9 urgent 10 cautious
11 conceptual, conceptualize 12 diagnosis

5 1 similar do not have a fixed place to live
different **a nomad** is a member of a tribe that wanders from place to place to find food for its cattle; **a gipsy** is a member of a dark-skinned race of people, originally from India, but now living in many parts of Europe. These people move about in caravans.

52

2 similar   both help to solve crimes
  different   **a fingerprint** is the mark made by the finger when pressed
             on a smooth surface and it may serve as a clue
3 similar   both are small containers
  different   **a canister** is a small box, usu metal, for holding tea, coffee,
             tobacco, etc
4 similar   both perceived by the ears
  different   **a noise** is a loud and unpleasant sound, esp confused and
             disagreeable
5 similar   both connected with travel
  different   a flight is a trip or journey made by plane
6 similar   both accidental and dangerous
  different   **fall** is to descend through the air, **crash**, used for cars,
             planes, etc, is to hit sth else very hard, causing damage
7 similar   not dying
  different   **survive** is to experience an event which would be likely to
             kill one, but to go on living
8 similar   connected with getting back to health from illness
  different   **cure** is cause sb to get better; **recover** is get better
9 similar   perceive sounds through the ear
  different   **listen** is actively try to perceive sounds
10 similar   do sth good in a bad situation
  different   **save** is help in such a way that damage or loss of life
             is avoided

6   **stray** [+ which has gone away from the right place]
     inscrutable [+ incapable of being understood or interpreted]
     muster [+ bring or come together] [+ for a common purpose]
     flaunt [+ make visible] [+ in an ostentatious and boastful manner]
     sway [+ produce an effect which makes one turn from a given course]
     assemble [+ bring or come together]
     shield [+ actively repel what threatens or attacks]
     canister [+ small box] [+ usu of metal]
     proclaim [+ make known] [+ by stating explicitly] [+ formally,
                 solemnly, officially]
     luminous [+ able to glow in the dark]
     uncanny [+ very strange] [+ possibly of supernatural origin]
     expose [+ lay open, uncover, take away protection] [+ make visible]
     stamp [+ put one's foot/feet down] [+ with force]

7   1 noise, event, number, man out   2 need, message   3 time, age,
     customer   4 circumstances, person, smile   5 comment, critic   6 face,
     experience, phenomenon   7 foundation, belief   8 story, adventure,
     experience, tale   9 handkerchief, cloth, shirt   10 apparition, tumour

8   1 a step up to the door of a building   2 one who amuses an audience as a
     profession   3 the silky covering which a caterpillar makes for itself
     before it changes into a butterfly   4 story, description, explanation
     5 seeming to see or hear something which is not really present   6 ghost
     or other non-material being   7 a person who studies astrology, the art of
     telling what will happen in the future by noting the position of the stars
     8 legs and arms   9 the state of being separate from and uninfluenced by
     surroundings   10 rebirth of the soul in a new body, so as to have another
     life after death   11 close connection, being similar to   12 a supposed

power that controls and decides everything and which cannot be resisted
13 tending to fill or pass through every part   14 revive, bring back to life
15 announce the coming of an event   16 despise, consider oneself
superior to

9   to **show** a wide knowledge of vocabulary   to **protect** one's health, a
child from bad influences, one's eyes from the sun   to **declare** war   to
collect one's thoughts   to **safeguard** one's health   to **pronounce** them
man and wife   to **flaunt** one's newly acquired riches   to **shield** one's eyes
from the sun   to **proclaim** peace, independence   to **defend** a thesis, one's
rights   to **expose** one's skin to the sun   to **announce** one's engagement
to **display** a wide knowledge of vocabulary   to **pick up** radio signals   to
gather flowers, mushrooms

10   1 stray   2 conducted   3 exhibiting   4 mustered   5 deceased   6 retrieved   7 luminous   8 crashed   9 resent   10 deranged   11 ward
12 stamping

11   1 similar   produce an effect
      different   **influence** results in a change in action, attitude, nature
      2 similar   to go into sth
      different   **penetrate** suggests difficulty, or piercing sth in order to
                 enter
      3 similar   attitude of mind
      different   **hope** is to want sth to be the case; **believe** is have it in one's
                 mind that sth is the case
      4 similar   be concerned for sth/sb
      different   **worry** is to feel concern without taking action; **care for** is to
                 look after
      5 similar   desire sth to be so
      different   **long for** is want very much
      6 similar   movement with one foot
      different   **stamp** is to step with force
      7 similar   produce an effect
      different   **impress** is have a strong effect, whereas **sway** is to turn from
                 a given course of action or opinion
      8 similar   make visible
      different   **display** is to show off to advantage, to attract attention
      9 similar   both products of energy
      different   **heat** is more intense than **warmth**
      10 similar   things which are said
      different   **an utterance** is any form of speech, **a sentence** is a syntactic
                 unit containing at least one verb and one noun
      11 similar   both study the mind
      different   **a psychiatrist** is a doctor who specializes in mental dis-
                 orders, **a psychologist** studies how the mind works
      12 similar   very strange
      different   **weird** is possibly of supernatural origin; **eerie** is causing
                 superstitious fear

12   1 to cross one's mind   2 to spread butter on bread, soil in a flowerbed
3 to channel water through a ditch   4 to gather strength, speed, information, one's wits   5 to shake fruit from a tree, a carpet   6 to muster
one's courage, one's resources   7 to dig a hole, the ground

13   1 showed   2 display   3 retrieved   4 find   5 assembled   6 collected
7 kill   8 slaughtered   9 emanating   10 sway

Revision exercises

R1   1 one who uses his strength to frighten and hurt those who are not so strong   2 an unexpected or contemptuous refusal   3 picture used in teaching young children   4 problem which arises in taking a particular course of action   5 feeling of happiness and contentment   6 power to do things, cleverness   7 a condition, especially a bad one   8 complete or infinite knowledge   9 freedom from work   10 the quality or fact of deserving praise, excellence   11 reply to an attack with similar action or speech   12 be used in the place of sth, because better   13 quarrel on purpose with one individual, rather than others   14 insist on one's rights   15 get on well with sb   16 refuse to retreat in a battle, or to give in to another in an argument   17 watch carefully   18 become more important, increase in importance   19 on hands and knees   20 purchase by instalments, instalment buying

R2   1 meeting, marriage   2 room, crowd, person   3 antique, picture, sorrow   4 Gothic style, oak beams, impression   5 clothes, talk, cook   6 behaviour, person   7 person, smell, behaviour   8 illness, fire place   9 room, office, garden, house appearance   10 glance, look, manner, smile, movement

R3   1 counterculture   2 bully   3 felt-tip pen   4 fringe benefits   5 fussy   6 dusk   7 foreman   8 subordinates   9 file   10 shipyard

R4   1 **false**   see Student's Book, grid 6, p 108
2 **get**   see Student's Book, grid 7, p 110
3 **damage** see Student's Book, grid 2, p 25

R5   1 self-esteem   2 lovely   3 grimy   4 reluctant   5 catastrophes   6 harm   7 impaired   8 damaged   9 hurts   10 injured   11 sturdy   12 forestall

R6   **drab** [+ cheerless] [+ dark in colour]
ward off [+ of undesirable things] [+ keep at a distance]
restore [+ to a former condition] [+ bring back]
phony [+ always intended to deceive] [+ arousing suspicion]
strip [+ take off/away covering or furnishing]
wallow [+ roll about] [+ usu in mud, dust, or water] [+ take excessive
       pleasure in]
drudgery [+ tedious] [+ work]
retain [+ to continue to have] [+ stresses the possibility of losing]
stealthy [+ careful not to be recognized or caught]
glimmer [+ send out a soft light]

R7   − intense   + intense

like	feel affection for	be attached to	be fond of	love	be in love with	be infatuated	adore

R8   1 similar   having a good appearance
    different   **smart** is fashionable or formally dressed or clean and tidy;
    well-groomed is clean and tidy, showing great attention to
    small details of one's appearance, usu of women only
    2 similar   to run
    different   **scamper** is usually of small or young animals or children,
    scurry is run with short, quick steps, as if in a hurry
    3 similar   lowering one's body
    different   **to squat** is to sit on the heels with the knees bent
    4 similar   to make impure
    different   **to contaminate** is to make impure or poisonous by contact
    with harmful matter, eg bacteria, poisonous gas, or radio-
    activity; **to pollute** is to make dirty by introduction of
    harmful waste-products
    5 similar   (when used attributively), someone who helps but does not
    want to
    different   (when used predicatively), **unwilling** means not doing,
    reluctant implies that sb did it, but without wanting to
    6 similar   sth is found in a certain place
    different   **infest** is be present in great numbers, usu of sth bad
    7 similar   sth one can do
    different   **responsibility** is sth one should do, has an obligation to do
    liability is a legal obligation
    8 similar   trying to stop sth bad
    different   **respite** is temporary rest from sth bad, **relief** is an attempt
    to improve conditions
    9 similar   what one does to earn one's living
    different   **profession** requires higher education or special training
    10 similar   work
    different   **toil** is long and tiring work; **grind** is tedious, long, and
    routine work
    11 similar   hiding
    different   **secret** is known to no one; **secretive** is not telling anybody
    what one is doing or thinking
    12 similar   avoid
    different   **duck** is to avoid an approaching object by a quick down-
    ward movement; **evade** is to avoid doing sth one is supposed
    to do by deception
    13 similar   to bring back
    different   **to revive** is to bring back to life; **to restore** is to bring back
    to a former condition
    14 similar   to continue to have
    different   **to retain** stresses the possibility of losing

R9   1 see Student's Book, grid 4, p 106
    2 see Student's Book, grid 4b, p 127
    3 see Student's Book, grid 3, p 105

R10   1 gazed 2 bring up   3 limited   4 growing   5 breeding   6 shifting
    7 change   8 resume   9 gentle   10 resumed   11 mild   12 lenient
    13 permissive   14 indulgently   15 brought   16 up   17 claim
    18 overstate   19 grown   20 cope with   21 dealing with   22 tackling
    23 bully   24 utmost   25 adolescence   26 envious   27 to be cajoled

28 grumbled   29 strain   30 pitfalls   31 esteem   32 constricting
33 sly   34 blackmail   35 shrewd   36 frequent   37 dubious
38 sampling   39 giddy

Unit 9

1   1 to earn respect, admiration   to cause others to respect or admire one
    to earn one's living, £5,000 a year   to be paid money in return for
    work
    2 to break one's leg, a record   to cause sth to come into pieces
    to break sb's heart   to cause great sorrow to
    to break the news to somebody   tell, make known
    to break sb's spirit   break sb's resistance
    to break the law   fail to obey
    to break one's word   not do what one has said one will do
    3 to grasp a rope, sb's hand   to hold on to with the hand
    to grasp an argument   understand
    4 to spend money   pay out
    to spend time, one's leisure   use time
    5 to build a house, a railway   construct
    to build in a cupboard   to add to a construction
    to build up a good reputation, a fortune   make steadily and gradually
    6 the roof leaks   allows water to enter
    the news leaked out   has become known in spite of efforts to keep it
    secret
    7 the tent collapsed   fell down
    our plans collapsed   did not succeed
    8 susceptible to flattery   easily moved or influenced by
    a susceptible young girl   easily influenced, esp ignorant of evil and so
    unprotected against it

2   1 a camera, the height of the cutter, a television   2 a car, cigarettes,
    books from a library   3 a meeting, a series of tests, a research project, a
    shop   4 all my chocolates, my new pen from my desk   5 a film, a
    play, a school, a project   6 the apple from sb's hand, at the purse, an
    hour's sleep   7 new social conditions, a cooler climate   8 rooms,
    flats, houses, shops   9 different social conditions, the rules, the usages of
    society   10 dresses, suits, car, boat, plane   11 sb's hand, a rope, an
    opportunity   12 the rope, sb's arm   13 fits of depression, change
    14 flattery, the cold, bad influences

3   1 similar   to make a hole in the earth, usu with a spade
      different   **delve** is to turn over and over, searching for sth
    2 similar   to look for sth
      different   **forage** is to look for food in an uncultivated region
    3 similar   steal
      different   **lift** is for small-sized things, **swipe** is very colloquial
    4 similar   make sure an organization functions
      different   **manage** is take decisions and make work for others; **super-
      vise** is make sure others are fulfilling a task set by sb else
    5 similar   **an item** is used by sb other than its owner, without payment
      different   **lend** is allow sb to use sth, **borrow** is to use sth of sb else

6 similar   **an item** is used by sb other than its owner, for payment
  different   **hire** is both allow sb to use sth, and use sth belonging to sb else, and usu is used for movable objects; **rent** is use sth belonging to sb else, and is usu used for fixed property
7 similar   take hold of suddenly and forcibly
  different   **snatch** is quickly, **grab** is roughly
8 similar   noisy disturbances involving many people
  different   **riot** may indicate a physical fight, **rumpus** may indicate a verbal quarrel
9 similar   state where things are not as they were before
  different   **upheaval** suggests disorganisation, but things may return to their previous state; **change** indicates that their new state is different
10 similar   people or animals which live in certain places
  different   **inhabitants** is used with an area or region, and indicates permanency; **resident** is used usu for people, for types of housing and may be permanent or temporary
11 similar   both describe anti-social people
  different   **a thug** is a large, tough man, capable of violent behaviour towards others; **a criminal** is sb proved to have committed a crime

4   1 multiplication   2 distinction   3 lodging   4 implication   5 dweller, dwelling   6 basement, basis   7 growth   8 finding   9 destruction   10 disturbance   11 combatant   12 operator, operation   13 digger   14 settlement   15 delivery   16 plasterer   17 intervention   18 roofer   19 forester   20 insecurity   21 riches, the rich   22 persistence

5   1 a line and a hook, or a net   2 some land, a plough or a tractor   3 a tape-measure, a thermometer   4 a gun, or a trap   5 food and drink   6 a car, a bus, a lorry, etc and a driving licence   7 money, a lease   8 the ability to do similar things   9 paper, an envelope, a pen, a stamp, a post box   10 brains   11 good qualifications, experience, good references, ability   12 money, a plan, bricks, stone, wood, glass, tiles etc

6   1 prospective   2 endeavour   3 released   4 chased   5 face   6 raid   7 deluge   8 lodging   9 foraged   10 ploy   11 blandly, bluntly   12 elaborate

7   1 up   2 without   3 small   4 mixed   5 habits   6 reached   7 shaft   8 spread

8   1 similar   both involve talking between at least two people
     different   **a chat** is informal, unstructured conversation, often between people who know each other, or who are meeting informally
  2 similar   both people who may commit a crime
     different   **a prowler** is looking for the opportunity to steal sth; **a thief** has already stolen sth
  3 similar   buildings not intended for human habitation
     different   **a barn** is for storing animal foodstuffs on a farm; **a stable** is where horses are kept

4 similar　both are connected with money
　different　**income** is the sum of money one gains either in return for work, or as interest on invested money
5 similar　both geographical features involving water
　different　**a creek** is a branch or inlet leading from a river, usu near the sea
6 similar　both imply disorder and confusion
　different　**upheaval** is change and confusion resulting from a specific event, and suggests attempts made to end the situation; whereas **riot** is specifically a deliberate public disturbance involving many people
7 similar　areas containing many houses
　different　**a suburb** is a residential area close to, or joined to, a large town
8 similar　divisions of agricultural land
　different　**meadow** is smaller, and usu planted with grass
9 similar　both build houses
　different　**a mason** constructs with stone; **a plasterer** gives interior walls a smooth finish by applying plaster
10 similar　come into physical contact with another person
　different　**nudge** is push slightly, usu to attract attention; **push** is apply strong pressure against a person or object, usu to make it move
11 similar　taking sth which does not belong to one
　different　**pilfer** is steal small things, or small quantities
12 similar　cause events to happen
　different　**direct** is tell others what to do; **conduct** is carry out a complex piece of work

9　1 substance, person, situation　2 plans, design, dinner　3 secretary, workman, officer　4 accident, wound, mistake　5 decision, person, course of action　6 gases, fumes, smell　7 appetite, meal, construction 8 cleaning, investigation, survey　9 argument, system, situation 10 work, lecture, job　11 character, honour, title　12 worker, face, looks

10　**apt**　see Student's Book, grid 8, p 170
　　riot　see Student's Book, grid 2, p 165

11　1 grasp　2 tedious　3 nudged　4 delved　5 comprised　6 fee 7 resides　8 inhabited

12　**adapt**　see Student's Book, unit 9, grid 4, p 167
　　inhabitant　see Student's Book, grid 1, p 165

Revision exercises

R1　**fastidious** [+ imposing near perfection]
　　salary [+ paid monthly] [+ usu by cheque]
　　mock [+ intended as a substitute for the real thing] [+ made in close imitation of sth else]
　　shirk [+ avoid] [+ usu work or duty]
　　toil [+ work] [+ long] [+ tiring]
　　avert [+ prevent from happening] [+ or undesirable things]

compassion [+ sensitive, emotional reaction] [+ share and understand the distress and misfortune of another] [+ desire to help and spare]
flounder [+ stumble or struggle] [+ helplessly and without progress]
glisten [+ reflect light] [+ not very bright, as from a wet surface]
furtive [+ careful not to be seen]
divest [+ take away] [+ distinction or mark of special privilege]
underhand [+ deceitful] [+ not open or straightforward]

R2 1 sabbatical (leave) 2 greedy 3 awe 4 sanity 5 dainty 6 bill
7 luminous 8 variable 9 Crusades

R3 1 similar   to avoid sth by physical movement
          different   **duck** is lower one's body; **dodge** is used figuratively for avoiding sth one should do
        2 similar   take sth off or away
          different   **strip** suggests making completely bare, often by pulling, tearing or scraping (except in the case of clothes); **divest** is take off outer covering, usu clothes; it is also used for removal of honours, privileges, etc
        3 similar   tell everyone good things about oneself
          different   **brag** often implies that the things are not true
        4 similar   light being visible
          different   **glimmer** is to be the source of a very faint light; **shimmer** is to reflect flashes of bright light
        5 similar   not draw attention to one's good achievements or characteristics
          different   **belittle** oneself suggests actually saying one is less good than the fact
        6 similar   a thing so described is what it appears to be
          different   **genuine** also suggests sincerity and honesty
        7 similar   the start of sth
          different   **onset** is only for bad things
        8 similar   members of the legal profession
          different   **solicitors** advise on legal matters and draw up legal documents, they cannot appear in the high court
        9 similar   types of deception or ways of persuading sb to do sth
          different   **trick** always implies deception; **gimmick** is an unusual or novel item, usu designed to draw attention to sth and make people want to spend money on it

R4 1 **show**   see Student's Book, grid 2, p 145
        2 **gather** see Student's Book, grid 6, p 149

R5 1 affinity 2 deranged 3 apparition 4 refused 5 threaten
6 shuddered 7 munched 8 fussy 9 peering 10 merchandise
11 gentle 12 outset

R6 1 flat tyre: not inflated   flat bottom: even, level bottom   flat surface: smooth, even, and level   flat beer: beer without sparkle, no longer bubbling with gas   flat refusal: plain and absolute   flat note: below the true pitch
2 plain English: clear, simple, easy to understand   plain food: simple, not rich or complicated, easy to digest   plain cooking: results in plain food   plain talk: frank, sincere, direct

3 dry wood/clothes: not wet   dry well: one without water in it   dry
bread: without butter   dry wine: not having a sweet taste   dry book:
dull and uninteresting   dry subject: dull and uninteresting   dry humour:
quiet and subtle   dry facts: plain and undisguised   dry cough: result of
throat irritation, sounds and feels as if the throat is dry
4 simple machine: easy to operate, performing an easy task   simple sentence: having only one finite verb   simple food: plain, not elaborate
simple style: plain, uncomplicated, not decorated   the simple life: a
healthy way of living, without sophisticated entertainment or social
meetings   simple peasant: humble, of low rank   simple forms of life:
animals which are very little evolved
5 rich furnishings: expensive and elaborate   rich cake: containing much
fat, butter, sugar, etc   rich diet: very varied, with elaborate dishes containing expensive items   rich colours: full, deep   rich voice: deep   rich
joke: very humorous
6 a small town/sum: little, not large   small business: of limited size,
having limited capital   small talk: conversation on subjects of little importance   small eater: who eats very little
7 steady rate: a regular, uniform, not changing   steady speed: regular, not
changing   steady worker: works hard and at the same speed all the time
steady progress: regular, uniform, not changing   steady boyfriend: one
with whom one spends time on a regular basis

R7   pinch, sham, brag, shipshape, shift, crow, grouse, squat, phony, fussy,
bellyache, flabbergast, lift, grind, scrap, ghastly, turn down

R8   1 similar   types of arguing
           different   **to bicker** is to argue about unimportant things, **to wrangle**
                        is to enter into a lengthy argument
        2 similar   express one's discontent with sth
           different   **grumble** suggests lengthy complaining about unspecified
                        things
        3 similar   contribute to the progress of sth, or sb
           different   **advance** may also mean make progress
        4 similar   affect with wonder
           different   **astound** suggests strong reaction, to the point that the per-
                        son affected cannot think or act
        5 similar   express amusement
           different   **smirk** is a kind of smile expressing contempt, **chuckle** is a
                        quiet low laugh
        6 similar   able to think efficiently and form good judgements
           different   **cunning** suggests ability to deceive
        7 similar   connected with material wealth
           different   **opulent** means displaying great riches and usually refers
                        to the external signs of being rich
        8 similar   insufficient
           different   **scanty** is used for size or quantity of sth
        9 similar   members of the human race, usu a group having common
                        attributes
           different   **folk** refers to unspecified groups and is colloquial

R9   1 rate, speed, worker, progress, boyfriend   2 laws, judge, parents,
teachers, attitude   3 fire-place, impression, Gothic style, prehistoric finds
4 hazards, disease   5 existence, room, neighbourhood, building, old cur-

tains   6 person, smile, nature   7 existence, society, family, lifestyle
8 medicine, mixture, drink (coll), drug   9 politician, diplomat, move,
person, critic   10 teacher, society, legislation, sexual behaviour, morals
11 pace, work, temper, disposition, surface   12 village, garden, little
house, kitchen, room, study, office   13 natural resources, salary, food,
allowance   14 passport, money, letters, document   15 man, room, conditions, upbringing, treatment, regime   16 fire-place, Gothic style, gun,
robbery, cream, smile

R10   1 **ward off**   see Student's Book, grid 5, p 110
2 **spurn**   see Student's Book, grid 5, p 47
3 **revive**   see Student's Book, grid 4, p 109

R11   1 pronounced   2 assembled   3 resuscitated   4 overt   5 unwilling
6 disagreeable   7 hazardous   8 predict   9 averted   10 careless
11 shift   12 attracted   13 quivering   14 compassion

R12

Unit 10

1   1 a rough length of wood as it comes from the tree   2 a person who
stops taking part in something (esp for academic courses)   3 a person
who eats no meat   4 a red precious stone   5 cups, plates etc made from
clay   6 stewed apples, often eaten together with roast pork   7 a person
who pays attention to small, unimportant details, usu to complain about
them, or cause trouble   8 amount of time, space, money, allowed for cal-
culations to be inexact   9 completely full   10 a mean, meagre salary
coll   11 outside an area which one may lawfully enter   12 about to

begin a war   13 making one very unhappy and disappointed   14 for
many years continously   15 to go back along a route one has already
passed along   16 without shoes or socks   17 change jobs frequently
18 make shorter by removing what is unnecessary   19 taking two factors
X and Y, take a decision which takes both equally into consideration
20 to walk in the country, for pleasure or exercise

2   roam [+ without any special purpose] [+ on foot or by other means]
        [+ quite a long way]
     verge [+ narrow strip of land beside a road]
     dawdle [+ spend more time than is necessary or usual in doing sth]
     coast [+ area of land near the sea]
     stroll [+ going] [+ on foot] [+ a short distance] [+ in an unhurried
        manner] [+ relaxed]
     brink [+ line or part of a line marking the limit of sth] [+ usu of water]
     loiter [+ for no reason or no apparent reason] [+ stay in one place]
     rim [+ line or part of a line marking the limit of sth] [+ often circular or
        curved]
     bank [+ land bordering a river or canal]
     dillydally [+ spend more time than is necessary or usual in doing sth]
        [+ by playing around with irrelevant and unimportant things]
        [+ in a silly way]
     brim [+ flat part which extends round the face on a hat] or [+ upper
        limits, usu of a container when full]
     bounds [+ the limits of sth]

3   1 thief, troubles, cash   2 mob, passions, sea   3 person, child,
     little puppy   4 knife, pin, features   5 affairs, questions, problems
     6 throat, voice, cry   7 day, ground, war   8 considerations, questions,
     matters   9 neck, old hen, joint (of meat)   10 person, experience, nature
     11 salary, present, helping of ice-cream   12 cream, milk, ideas, material,
     vegetables

4   1 foam   2 ribbon   3 rucksack   4 mansion   5 teenager   6 scrap
     7 immerse   8 commute

5   1 fly   see Student's Book, grid 6, p 191
     2 stare   see Student's Book, grid 7, p 192

6   1 glowed   2 hoarse   3 flurry   4 choke   5 rustle   6 turbulent
     7 moss   8 verge

7   1 verge   *lit* narrow strip of land beside a road
                  fig point just before the beginning of sth
     2 flock   *lit* number of sheep
                  fig followers (esp of a religious leader)
     3 border   *lit* dividing line between two countries
                  fig imaginary line between two situations or states of mind
     4 fade   *lit* lose brightness slowly
                  fig lose distinctness slowly
     5 margin   *lit* part not written on at two sides of the page
                  fig amount of error allowed
     6 prune   *lit* to reduce in size by removing parts of trees
                  fig (of something written) considerably reduce in size by
                       taking out unnecessary parts

7 brink *lit* line marking the limit of sth, usu with a steep side
    fig point just before beginning sth
8 swarm *lit* colony of bees
    fig large numbers (of people)

8 1 similar   to move by stepping forward
    different   **trudge** is walk wearily and with effort
   2 similar   movement of the head
    different   **nod** is tilt the head forward and back again to show agreement; **bow** is tilt the head forward as a sign of sorrow, or respect
   3 similar   move fast
    different   **scurry** is move with quick short steps
   4 similar   heating food to prepare for eating
    different   **simmer** is cook slowly in water
   5 similar   moving round
    different   **bustle** is to move around a limited area, quickly and busily
   6 similar   result in pictorial images in the mind
    different   **envision** is see in imagination what might happen in the future
   7 similar   part of the body
    different   **ribs** are the bones attached to the spine which protect the heart and lungs; chops are pieces of animal meat each cut to include one rib
   8 similar   marked depression in the surface of the earth
    different   **pit** is not natural, and must be quite large, at least 20 cm across
   9 similar   places for sitting
    different   **a pew** is a long wooden bench, fixed to the floor, found in a church
  10 similar   noises
    different   **rustle** is a gentle sound of movement, eg of leaves

9 1 on   2 at   3 at   4 at   5 out   6 into   7 down/along   8 round
   9 over   10 away   11 on, of   12 on

10 1 **flock**   see Student's Book, grid 3, p 189
    2 **border**   see Student's Book, grid 1, p 187
    3 **prune**   see Student's Book, grid 4, p 194

11 1 strolled   2 edge   3 loitered   4 soared   5 flitted   6 hovered
    7 stared   8 gape   9 petty   10 surpassed   11 brink

12 | **American** | **British** |
| --- | --- |
| colored | coloured |
| neighborhood | neighbourhood |
| neighbors | neighbours |
| enamored | enamoured |
| vapors | vapours |
| marvelous | marvellous |

13 wise old pines: wise normally goes with human subjects
    hawks and falcons bulleted by: bullets are from guns
    watching him rocket into the darkness: rockets are missiles which go into space

our surburbanized muscles: suburbanized normally describes the country
everything flowed seasonally: seasonlly used to imply regularity
a cold breath of winter: breath is [+ animate]
those strange ribbons of colored cloth around: ties around their necks
soon we were immersed in a dinner: immerse normally means be or cause
    to be surrounded by a liquid
his Monday night classes were magnetizing some 2,000 students:
    magnetize = attract a metal by electrical force
partake of the Farm's life: partake usu collocates with meal
a pink, white and red fantasy: a fantasy is a story in the imagination
moss-bearded prophets: moss is a plant

Revision exercises

R1   1 work   2 take   3 dangerous   4 avoid   5 complain   6 lawyer
           7 look   8 smile   9 quarrel   10 fly   11 laugh   12 shake   13 steal

R2   **stray** dogs, cattle   **weird** animal, experience, circumstances   **odd** jobs,
    smile, times, circumstances   **enigmatic** person, smile, circumstances
    uncanny experience, circumstances   **announce** that the price of the meat
    will rise, sb to be the winner   **declare** sb to be the winner   **proclaim** sb
    king   **pronounce** sb dead, sb to be the winner

R3   1 a meeting, research, an experiment   2 a camera, the height of the
    cutter   3 dresses, suits, typewriters, cars   4 a blow, the police, taxes,
    the issue   5 boats, planes, ships, helicopters   6 balloons, tyres, air-beds
    7 rooms, flats, houses, shops   8 a secret, the truth   9 one's lunch, a
    bedroom, losses   10 a line, a verse, sb's words, a price   11 wild animals,
    a blow, evil, an attack   12 a field, land   13 a competitor, an attempt to
    do sth   14 rooms, flats, houses, shops, cars

R4   1 similar   avoiding sth
      different   **shirk** is to avoid doing sth one is supposed to do, or for
                which one has a responsibility
    2 similar   prevent sth undesirable from happening
      different   **ward off** is keep away, whereas **avert** is prevent from
                happening, of events
    3 similar   display sth in public
      different   **expose** is show sth which has not been seen before; **flaunt** is
                draw everyone's attention to sth, because one is proud of it
    4 similar   produce an effect on sb
      different   **sway** is produce an effect which makes sb turn from one
                course of action to another
    5 similar   bring or come together
      different   **muster** suggests a common purpose
    6 similar   make known by stating explicitly
      different   **pronounce** is only speaking, and its use is confined to for-
                mal situations like official declarations
    7 similar   money in return for work
      different   **wages** are paid in cash, usually weekly; **a salary** is paid by
                cheque, or directly into a bank account, usu monthly
    8 similar   both send out light
      different   a luminous substance sends out light in the dark

          9 similar   unusual, unexpected, not normal
            different **uncanny** suggests supernatural causes, or something which
                       cannot easily be explained
         10 similar   not rich, ornamented or patterned
            different **simple** can also mean uncomplicated or easy, or (of people)
                       not clever
         11 similar   likely to undergo
            different **prone** is usually used where the event cannot be avoided
         12 similar   describe things which achieve their purpose
            different **efficient** means using the least effort and time to achieve the
                       result

R5   1 to land   2 to look down on   3 to decline   4 to repair   5 to miss
         6 to advance   7 to borrow   8 to reveal, to find   9 physical
         10 prone, susceptible   11 small, tiny, petite, diminutive   12 inward
         13 trivial, unimportant, petty   14 scarce, sparse, frugal   15 overt,
         open, obvious   16 permanent, consistent   17 inflexible, rigid, fixed
         18 fake, counterfeit, pretend, false   19 rough, bumpy   20 green,
         wooded, fertile   21 mild, kind, easy   22 interest, concern, care

R6   1 riots   2 tramps   3 traders, dealers   4 surveyors   5 plumbers
         6 moths   7 masons   8 plasterers

R7   1 worker   person who works
          2 workable   of a plan or project which can be put into practice
          3 workless   of sb who has no job
          4 workman   person who works manually
            seaman   person who works on the sea
          5 seaside   area of land near the sea
          6 sea mile   measure of distance used in navigation
          7 workload   amount of work to be done during a given period or by an
                       individual
          8 workshop   small room where one or a few people make or repair
                       mechanical or wooden goods
          9 seasick   ill because of the motion of the waves at sea
         10 seafood   edible fish
         11 workday   day when one works
         12 seashore   strip of land immediately bordering on the sea
         13 seaweed   plants which grow in the sea
         14 workshy   of sb who avoids work
         15 seagull   popular name for several varieties of birds which live near
                       the sea

R8   1 leapt   2 hampered   3 prowler   4 delivers   5 quest   6 decline
         7 destination   8 odd   9 steadily   10 drab   11 gazed   12 shining

R9   1 public transport   2 lawyer   3 pavement   4 lift   5 flat   6 car
         7 chequer board   8 veterinary surgeon or vet   9 estate agent
         10 rucksack   11 ring road   12 to prune   13 to grow   14 to reach
         15 to choke

R10 (the figures in brackets refer to the Unit)
         1 lunatic asylum (7)   2 bedside reading (5)   3 footprints (10)
         4 heart-felt (3)   5 water table (3)   6 deathbed (8)   7 motorbike (8)
         8 fingerprint (8)   9 shop assistant (6)   10 insurance adjuster (6);

insurance agent (9)   11 snow flurry (10)   12 land developers (9);
land pressure (9); landlocked (10); landowner (9)   13 estate agent (9)
14 neon light (9)   15 car washer (6); car park (9)   16 mountain
man (10); mountain stream (10); mountain top (10)   17 farmhouse (9)
18 telephone lineman (repair man) (9)   19 tax assessor (9)   20 health
officials (9)

R11   1 support   2 understand   3 strange   4 secret   5 weird   6 changed
7 penalty   8 defended   9 avoided   10 monotonous   11 spurned
12 arid   13 collected

R12   1 similar   change so as to meet new conditions
  different   **conform** needs the presence of already agreed conventions
2 similar   to take off covering
  different   **denude** is usu used for vegetation covering the land
3 similar   to try to catch sth/sb
  different   **chase** is to follow after at speed
4 similar   to get the use of sth from sb else in return for payment
  different   leasing always involves a long term and a definite contract
5 similar   to hold tight with the hand(s)
  different   **grab** suggests roughness
6 similar   to take sb else's property
  different   **pilfer** is used for small, unimportant things; **rip off** is
              colloquial
7 similar   cease to stand up
  different   **collapse** suggests lack of strength
8 similar   to say sth is not good
  different   **decry** is formal and slightly old-fashioned
9 similar   tell other people working on sth what to do
  different   a person supervising makes sure workers do a task ordered
              by sb else
10 similar   fights between small numbers of people
  different   a **brawl** is more violent than a **scrap**

R13   1 see Student's Book, grid 3, p 106
2 see Student's Book, grid 6, p 86
3 see Student's Book, grid 7, p 87
4 see Student's Book, grid 8, p 14
5 see Student's Book, grid 8, p 30

R14   1 job   2 vacancies   3 wages   4 glamorous   5 fussy   6 shirk
7 work   8 struggled   9 drab   10 clerical   11 secretarial   12 aiming
13 managerial   14 executive   15 salary   16 diversified   17 fought
18 avert   19 stability   20 accommodate   21 self-confidence
22 amend   23 strip off   24 query   25 design